# Innocent on Death Row

# The Darlie Lynn Routier Story

Copyright © 2014 by David J. Pietras

All rights reserved. No part of this publication may be reproduced, distributed, or transmitted in any form or by any means, including photocopying, recording, or other electronic or mechanical methods, without the prior written permission of the publisher, except in the case of brief quotations embodied in critical reviews and certain other noncommercial uses permitted by copyright law. For permission requests, write to the publisher, addressed "Attention: Permissions Coordinator," at the web site below.

http://mrdavepp.wix.com/davidpietras

Cover design by David Pietras

ISBN-13: 978-1495228018
ISBN-10: 1495228010

1 2 3 4 5 6 7 8 9 10 14

# Preface

Darlie Lynn Routier

In 1997, a court found Darlie Lynn Routier guilty of probably the worst of human crimes: killing two of her natural children in cold-blood. Motive is still a mystery, but the prosecution painted her as a shrewish, materialistic young woman who, sensing her lavish lifestyle crumbling, slew her two sons Damon and Devon in a mad attempt to resuscitate her and her husband's personal economy.

The following story relates the events of the murder and those leading up to her sensational trial, resulting in her conveyance to death row in Dallas, where she awaits death through lethal injection. The evidence against Darlie was damaging and, in retrospect, her defending counsel had little hope for her acquittal.

But, recent findings in her case have cast a doubt over her guilt at least over the legalities that brought her thumbs down to death row. Therefore, the final chapter in this report is dedicated to the most recent controversy that may result in a new trial for Darlie Lynn Routier.

# Darlie

Blonde, hazel-eyed Darlie was born in Altoona, Pennsylvania, on January 4, 1970, the first-born child of Darlie and Larry Peck. Doted on as a child, her first encounter with the harshness of life occurred at seven years old, when her parents divorced and the domestic security she knew tilted. A year later, her mother remarried a man named Dennis Stahl and, as Darlie entered her teens, the family moved to the vastly different climate of Lubbock, Texas.

Darlie-First Grade
Darlie Routier was in first grade when this school photo was taken

Little Darlie and her siblings two natural and two step sisters got on together well and helped each other through the difficult transition of hometowns and schools. The toughest part of their young lives was having to endure their parents' constant squabbling and sometimes violent fighting. Eventually, the Stahl's marriage faded and Darlie's mother was once again in search of a new spouse and her girls were without a father figure. As Darlie entered her teens, the family moved to the vastly different climate of Lubbock, Texas.

Darlie at prom
Darlie Routier poses at her senior prom in Lubbock in 1987, when the future seemed full of promise.

She had met Darin in a Western Sizzlin' where her mother worked and so did Darin as a cook. The mother found him a bright, talkative good-looking boy with ambitious plans for his future; he would be, she figured, a good catch for her oldest daughter. Playing matchmaker, she introduced the two kids and by all reports it was love at first sight for both of them. The dark-haired tall boy with wavy hair flipped for the five-foot-three, heart-faced Lubbock belle with the big eyes. And she, in turn, for him.

Darin and Darlie in photo booth
Darin Routier and Darlie Peck were dating when this photo was snapped.

They dated in high school and continued to correspond after Darin, two years older than she, went away to a technical college in Dallas. A preface of things to come occurred at Darin's going-away party. There, according to a friend named, Darlie showed a possessive and cunning nature that lay hidden under her surface sweetness. Darlie was annoyed that she wasn't getting enough attention, so she left the party. Then she came back frantic, claiming that someone had tried to rape her. That ruse gave her just the attention that she craved.

Darin and Darlie formal portrait
A young Darin and Darlie Routier posed for this photo in the late 1980s.

After graduating high school, Darlie joined her boyfriend in Dallas where he had been hired as a technician at a computer chip company. Landing a job with the same firm, the couple lived together while saving their money until, in August of 1988, they married. The couple honeymooned first-class in Jamaica.

After moving to the Dallas area he began his own small company that tested electronic components and when he became a success in the early nineties they bought a nice house and spent thousands getting it just how they wanted. Darin bought a thirty-foot cabin cruiser and a 1982 Jaguar. They went a little wild with their money and Darlie bought new boobs and flashy jewelry.

The company that Darin started was called Testnec. In 2013 at the time of the writing of this story Testec is located in Lubbock, TX. It is still categorized under Electronic Parts and Equipment; county records show that this company has annual revenue of $75,000.

# Trouble in Paradise

Their first child was born on June 14, 1989 a healthy boy named Devon Rush to be followed by another son on February 19, 1991 Damon Christian. With two children and a home company that grew so fast that the owners found it necessary to buy space in an upscale office building, the Routiers' life seemed to be following the quality dream of the new American family.

Devon and Damon Routier

By 1992, their company had earned them a small fortune. The up-and-coming couple yearned to practice the prestige due them and had a house built in Dalrock Heights Addition, an affluent suburb of Rowlett, adjacent to Lake Ray Hubbard. This community of upper-class businessmen and women bragged crime-free streets and happy families.

The $130,000 two-story home of Georgian design resembled a miniature mansion with classic porch, colonial shutters and a working fountain on the front lawn.

5801 Eagle Drive

Complementing their new life, the family boasted a Jaguar, sitting waxed and gleaming in a circular driveway.

Routier family

Darlie was happy. And she was a very good mother, doting on her two children, living to celebrate the good times with them. At Christmas, their house was the most illumined, at Halloween their windows displayed more goblins than any other, at Thanksgiving the Routier's turkey was the largest and most flavorful. On the children's birthdays, Darlie threw gorgeous parties inviting classmates for an afternoon of frolic in their spacious entertainment center.

But, there was another side of Darlie, claim some who knew her a side that loved to show off to cover a low self-esteem. She reveled in materialism and impression, often to the point of the bizarre. When she decided to get breast implants, she opted for size EE like the kind women had in *Playboy* and *Penthouse*. When she bought clothes, they were revealing outfits she wore out for a night's dancing just to grab the attention of onlookers. Her wardrobe bills skyrocketed.

Darlie's detractors say that her need to be the flashiest, gaudiest eventually overcame everything else in her life including her children. Neighbors complained that Damon and Devon, not far past the toddler stage, were left unsupervised. And when she did attend to them, she often seemed bothered at having to take the time to do so. Her patience with them decreased.

Roots of domestic problems surfaced. Celebrants at a Christmas party silently watched as Darlie and Darin argued violently when Darlie danced too many times with another man. There were rumors of extramarital dating by both partners. But, the couple continued to play the surface charade, buying buying, buying. They bought a 27-foot cabin cruiser and a space at the dock to board it at the exclusive Lake Ray Hubbard Marina.

Friends who were aware of their problems were happy when Darlie became pregnant early in 1995; they counted on the new baby as the common denominator to re-new the couple's love for each other. But, after Drake was born on October 18, 1995, the mother suffered postpartum depression. Mood swings drew sudden tempers and dark rages.

Not helping matters was the state of their finances, which, despite good business profits from Testnec, did not meet the exorbitant lifestyle Darlie and Darin preferred to live and had grown used to. Ends suddenly did not meet.

Asserts Barbara Davis in *Precious Angels*: "Testnec would gross more than a quarter of a million dollars (in 1995). Almost $12,000 worth of new equipment was purchased for the flourishing business. The Routiers' tax return for the year indicated a gross income of $264,000. With a profit range of 40 percent, the couple netted a little over $100,000."

Darlie was unable to shed the weight gain she had acquired since her last pregnancy and grew increasingly antagonistic. She dropped diet pills that didn't work. A fact that, when the couple battled, Darin would remind her of, knowing he'd hit her tender spot

Cost-cutting measures ignored, spending sprees accelerating, their financial troubles deepened. The toll on their serenity was excruciating. Testnec was losing money and Darin was unable to pay himself the salary he required, nor pay Darlie anything at all for doing the books, which she had let go in her depression. Creditors fell upon them, demanding late bills. On Saturday, June 1, their bank denied them a much-needed loan of $5,000.

Darlie sporadically kept a diary. There were times she would attend to it daily, followed by long absences. On May 3, 1996, contemplating suicide, she wrote, *"Devon, Damon and Drake, I hope you will forgive me for what I am about to do. My life has been such a hard fight for a long time, and I just can't find the strength to keep fighting anymore. I love you three more than anything else in this world and I want all three of you to be healthy and happy and I don't want you to see a miserable person every time you look at me..."*

Darin walked in on her while she was writing and noticed the tears swelling in her eyes. She broke down and confessed the terrible thoughts of suicide that had been running hot through her brain. He held her and they talked long into the afternoon. By the end of the conversation, she had calmed. For one afternoon, they loved each other again.

A month later something snapped. And flushed up hell.

# June 6, 1996

Dawn had not yet arrived over the posh neighborhood of Dalrock Heights Addition, near Rowlett, Texas, and in a bird's eye view the usually safe-and-coddled environs of the upper-class community looked peaceful and tranquil before the new day. But, at 5801 Eagle Drive, discordance roared. Evil rampaged.

The first outsider to hear of the troubles raging within was Doris Trammell, night dispatcher for the Rowlett Police Department. She was surprised when the emergency phone rang at 2:31 a.m. troubles were few there, for it was the kind of community known as a safe haven from the rest of the world, a place to raise a family but her nonchalance was jolted. A hysterical female voice at the other end of the line was telling a terrible story.

The voice screamed, "Somebody broke in to our house...They just stabbed me and my children..." Trammell shocked upright in her chair, captured her senses, then tried to calm the woman, tried to get the details in as orderly manner as possible. But, the caller continued to scream panic-stricken into the mouthpiece from her home..."My little boys are dying! Oh my God, my babies are *dying*!"

Trammell's fingers scrambled for and punched the main police unit line; she side-mouthed into the microphone, "Stand by for medical emergency, woman and children stabbed!" then advised the woman at the other end to hold on while she summoned an ambulance. But the woman continued to sob and yelp, without hesitation, "My babies are dying! My babies are dying!"

"Ma'am, please calm down, tell me what's happened!" the dispatcher begged, but the woman was incoherent and Trammell grew more confounded. Drawing up her computer screen, she traced the call by its caller ID to a number belonging to a Darin and Darlie Routier (pronounced Roo-tear) at 5801 Eagle Drive. After several more pleas, Trammell convinced the party at the other end to subdue, to take a deep breath, to explain what was happening over there. The dispatcher still could not believe what she was hearing. *Murder in peaceful Rowlett?*

# A Terrible Scene

Darlie Routier, the caller, spurted, sobbed, gasped and moaned a terrible tale unheard of in the up-until-then pleasant, placid suburb. "While I was sleeping...me and my little boys were sleeping downstairs...someone came in...Stabbed my babies.... stabbed me...I woke up...I was fighting...he ran out through the garage...threw the knife down..."

"How old are your boys?" Trammell pursued, and learned that the injured children were six and five. Devon and Damon were their names. In the meantime, a squad had detected the emergency vehicle wired by Trammell and reported to the dispatcher it was on its way to the Routier address.

Twenty-eight-year-old Darin Routier had been awakened from sleep upstairs by his wife Darlie's screams and now rushed downstairs into the family's entertainment room. Before he had gone to bed hours earlier, the last he had seen of that den was a domestic scene: his children lying on the floor watching their big screen television and Darlie lying on the sofa near them, looking sexy in her Victoria's Secret nightshirt.

Now, his two boys, Devon and Damon, lay blood-soaked while Darlie, her nightshirt covered in blood, paced in a paroxysm of panic shouting at the police dispatcher into the portable phone. Says Barbara Davis in her book, *Precious Angels*, "He saw blood everywhere... Darin rushed to Devon's side (and) saw two huge gashes in his son's chest where the six-year-old had been stabbed repeatedly. Checking for a pulse and feeling none, he looked at Devon's face. Eyes wide open...stared vacantly back." He then turned towards the other boy, five-year-old Damon, lying near a wall, his back to the room. "A small amount of blood was oozing through the back of his shorts," writes Davis. "Damon's lungs rattled as he struggled to suck in air.

"Torn between two sons, the horrified father momentarily panicked, and then made the decision to begin cardiopulmonary resuscitation on the son who was still wearing his Power Rangers pajamas. Darin placed his hand over Devon's nose and breathed into his child's mouth. Blood sprayed back onto the father's face."

While Darin is trying to save his children's lives Darlie calls 911. Here are the transcripts from that call.

# 911 TRANSCRIPTS

Recorded by The Rowlett Police Department

June 6, 1996.

Transcript created by Barry Dickey

(*This transcript was done after the state "enhanced" the recording and is not accurate)

Time ID Conversation/Sounds

00:00:00 911 Operator #1

...Rowlett 911...what is your emergency..

00:01:19 Darlie Routier ...somebody came here...they broke in...

00:03:27 911 Operator #1 ...ma'am...

00:05:11 Darlie Routier ...they just stabbed me and my children...

00:07:16 911 Operator #1 ...what...

00:08:05 Darlie Routier ...they just stabbed me and my kids...my little boys...

00:09:24 911 Operator #1 ...who...who did...

00:11:12 Darlie Routier ...my little boy is dying...

00:11:25 RADIO ...(unintelligible) clear...

00:13:07 911 Operator #1 ...hang on ...hang on... hang on

00:15:03 Darlie Routier ...hurry... (unintelligible)...

00:16:01 911 Operator #1 ...stand by for medical emergency

00:18:11 Darlie Routier ...ma'am...

00:18:19 911 Operator #1 ...hang on ma'am...

00:21:26 Darlie Routier ...ma'am...

00:23:00 911 Operator #1 ...unknown medical emergency... 5801 Eagle Drive...

00:24:00 RADIO ...(unintelligible)...

00:26:24 Darlie Routier ...ma'am...

00:27:12 911 Operator #1 ...ma'am... I'm trying to get an ambulance to you... hang on a minute...

00:28:20 RADIO...(siren)...

00:29:13 Darlie Routier ...oh my God ...my babies are dying...

00:30:12 Darin Routier ...(unintelligible)...

00:31:09 911 Operator #1 ...what's going on ma'am...

00:32:13 Darlie Routier ...(unintelligible) ...oh my God...

00:33:49 RADIO ...(tone-signal broadcast)...

00:34:01 Background Voice ...(unintelligible)...

00:35:20 Darlie Routier ...(unintelligible) thought he was dead ...oh my God...

00:39:08 Darin Routier ...(unintelligible)...

00:39:29 Darlie Routier ...I don't even know (unintelligible)...

00:40:22 911 Operator #1 ...attention 901 unknown medical emergency 5801...

00:42:23 Darin Routier ...(unintelligible)...

00:43:15 Darlie Routier ...I don't even know (unintelligible)...

00:44:04 911 Operator #1 ...Eagle Drive ...Box 238 ...cross street Linda Vista and Willowbrook ...attention 901 medical emergency...

00:49:28 Darlie Routier ...who was breathing...

00:40:10 Darin Routier ...(unintelligible)...

00:51:15 Darlie Routier ...(unintelligible) are they still laying there (unintelligible)...

00:51:19 911 Operator #1 ...may be possible stabbing ...5801 Eagle Drive ...Box 238 ...cross street Linda Vista and Willowbrook...

00:55:06 Darlie Routier ...oh my God ...what do we do...

00:57:17 911 Operator #1 ...time out 2:32...

00:58:26 Darlie Routier ...oh my God...

00:58:28 911 Operator #1 ...stamp me a card Clint...

01:01:02 911 Operator #1 ...80...

01:01:16 RADIO ...(unintelligible)...

01:02:13 Darlie Routier ...oh my God...

01:03:05 RADIO ...(unintelligible)...

01:04:07 911 Operator #1 ...need units going towards 5801 Eagle Drive ...5801 Eagle Drive

01:04:07 Darlie Routier ...oh my God ...my baby's dead...

01:07:08 Darlie Routier ...Damon ...hold on honey...

01:08:11 Darin Routier ...(unintelligible)...

01:08:22 911 Operator #1 ...hysterical female on the phone...

01:10:03 Darlie Routier ...(unintelligible)...

01:10:10 Darin Routier ...(unintelligible)...

01:10:26 911 Operator #1 ...says her child has been stabbed

01:11:28 Darlie Routier ...I saw them Darin...

01:12:21 Darin Routier ...oh my God ...(unintelligible) ...came in here...

01:14:10 911 Operator #1 ...ma'am ...I need you to calm down and talk to me...

01:14:24 RADIO ...(unintelligible)...

01:16:25 Darlie Routier ...ok...

01:16:26 SOUND ...(unintelligible)...

01:17:12 911 Operator #1 ...twice Clint...

01:18:26 Darlie Routier ...didn't you get my address...

01:20:19 911 Operator #1 ...5801 Eagle...

01:22:00 Darlie Routier ...yes ...we need help...

01:22:03 RADIO ...(unintelligible) will be Enroute code...

01:24:20 Darlie Routier ...Darin...I don't know who it was...

01:24:23 911 Operator #1 ...2:33 code...

01:26:15 Darlie Routier ...we got to find out who it was...

01:27:12 911 Operator #1 ...ma'am...

01:28:04 911 Operator #1 ...ma'am listen ...listen to me...

01:29:27 Darlie Routier ...yes ...yes ...(unintelligible)...

01:30:23 RADIO ...(unintelligible) I'm clear ...do you need anything...

01:32:08 Darin Routier ...(unintelligible)...

01:32:20 Darlie Routier ...oh my God...

01:34:00 911 Operator #1 ...(unintelligible)...

01:34:22 911 Operator #1 ...do you take the radio Clint...

01:35:23 911 Operator #2 ...yes...

01:36:12 Darlie Routier ...oh my God...

01:36:25 911 Operator #1 ...I...ma'am...

01:38:03 Darlie Routier ...yes...

01:38:17 911 Operator #1 ...I need you to ...

01:38:23 RADIO ...(unintelligible) start that way (unintelligible)... will revise...

01:39:28 911 Operator #1 ...I need you to talk to me...

01:41:21 Darlie Routier ...what ...what ...what...

01:44:25 RADIO ...(unintelligible)...

01:44:28 Darlie Routier ...my babies are dead (unintelligible)...

01:46:20 RADIO ...go ahead and start that way ...siren code 4 ...advise...

01:47:10 Darlie Routier ...(unintelligible)...

01:48:03 Darlie Routier ...(unintelligible) do you want honey ...hold on (unintelligible)...

01:49:17 911 Operator #1 ...ma'am ...I can't understand you...

01:50:21 Darlie Routier ...yes...

01:51:18 911 Operator #1 ...you're going to have to slow down ...calm down ...and talk to me...

01:52:19 Darlie Routier ...I'm talking to my babies ...they're dying...

01:55:03 911 Operator #1 ...what is going on...

01:56:29 Darlie Routier ...somebody came in while I was sleeping ...me and my little boys were sleeping downstairs...

02:02:00 RADIO ...(unintelligible) I'll be clear...

02:02:20 Darlie Routier ...some man ...came in ...stabbed my babies ...stabbed me ...I woke up ...I was fighting ...he ran out through the garage ...threw the knife down ...my babies are dying ...they're dead ...oh my God...

02:14:23 911 Operator #1 ...ok ...stay on the phone with me...

02:16:11 Darin Routier ...(unintelligible)...

02:17:06 Darlie Routier ...oh my God...

02:17:29 911 Operator #1 ...what happened (unintelligible) dispatch 901...

02:20:15 Darlie Routier ...hold on honey ...hold on...

02:22:01 911 Operator #1 ...(unintelligible) who was on (unintelligible)...

02:22:26 911 Operator #2 ...it was (unintelligible) the white phone...

02:23:08 Darlie Routier ...hold on...

02:25:26 911 Operator #2 ...they were wondering when we need to dispatch ...so I sent a double team...

02:25:28 Darlie Routier ...oh my God ...oh my God...

02:28:08 911 Operator #1 ...ok ...thanks...

02:28:21 Darlie Routier ...oh my God...

02:29:20 SOUND ...(unintelligible)...

02:30:01 Darlie Routier ...oh my God...

02:30:20 911 Operator #1 ...ma'am...

02:31:06 RADIO ...(unintelligible)...

02:31:14 911 Operator #1 ...who's there with you...

02:32:15 Darlie Routier ...Karen ...(unintelligible)...

02:33:15 911 Operator #1 ...ma'am...

02:34:06 Darlie Routier ...what...

02:38:11 911 Operator #1 ...is there anybody in the house ...

besides you and your children...

02:38:11 Darlie Routier ...no ...my husband he just ran downstairs ...he's helping me ...but they're dying ...oh my God ...they're dead...

02:43:24 911 Operator #1 ...ok ...ok ...how many little boys ...is it two boys...

02:46:06 Darin Routier ...(unintelligible)...

02:46:25 Darlie Routier ...there's two of 'em ...there's two...

02:48:18 RADIO ...what's the cross street on that address on Eagle...

02:50:15 Darlie Routier ...oh my God ...who would do this...

02:53:13 911 Operator #1 ...(unintelligible) listen to me ...calm down ...(unintelligible)...

02:53:21 Darlie Routier ...I feel really bad ...I think I'm dying...

02:55:06 RADIO ...228...

02:56:06 911 Operator #1 ...go ahead...

02:58:12 RADIO ...(unintelligible) address again (unintelligible)...

02:59:12 RADIO ...(unintelligible)...

02:59:22 Darlie Routier ...when are they going to be here...

03:00:22 911 Operator #1 ...5801 Eagle Drive ...5801 Eagle Drive...

03:03:28 Darlie Routier ...when are they going to be here...

03:03:29 911 Operator #1 ...going to be a stabbing...

03:05:20 Darlie Routier ...when are they going to be here...

03:06:20 911 Operator #1 ...ma'am ...they're on their way...

03:08:00 RADIO ...(unintelligible)...

03:08:08 Darlie Routier ...I gotta just sit here forever ...oh my God...

03:11:14 911 Operator #1 ...2:35...

03:12:05 Darlie Routier ...who would do this ...who would do this...

03:13:09 Darin Routier ...(unintelligible)...

03:14:26 911 Operator #1 ...(sounds of typing on computer keyboard)...

03:16:08 911 Operator #1 ...ma'am ...how old are your boys...

03:18:20 Darin Routier ...what...

03:19:03 911 Operator #1 ...how old are your boys...

03:20:04 RADIO ...(unintelligible)...

03:20:21 911 Operator #1 ...no...

03:21:01 Darlie Routier ...seven and five..

03:22:17 911 Operator #1 ...ok...

03:23:08 Darlie Routier ...oh my God ...oh my God ...oh ...he's dead...

03:29:02 911 Operator #1 ...calm down ...can you...

03:29:03 Darlie Routier ...oh God ...Devon no ...oh my God...

03:30:27 SOUND ...(dog barking)..

.

03:35:02 911 Operator #1 ...is your name Darlie...

03:36:11 Darlie Routier ...yes...

03:36:26 911 Operator #1 ...this is her...

03:37:09 911 Operator #1 ...is your husband's name Darin...

03:38:22 Darlie Routier ...yes ...please hurry ...God they're taking forever...

03:41:20 911 Operator #1 ...there's nobody in your house ...there was ...was...

03:44:05 911 Operator #1 ...you don't know who did this...

03:45:19 Police Officer ...look for a rag...

03:46:11 Darlie Routier ...they killed our babies...

03:48:03 Police Officer ...lay down ...ok ...just sit down ...(unintelligible)

03:51:11 911 Operator #1 ...(sounds of typing on computer keyboard)...

03:52:13 Darlie Routier ...no ...he ran out ...uh ...they ran out in the garage ...I was sleeping...

03:54:09 911 Operator #1 ...(unintelligible)...

03:56:19 Darlie Routier ...my babies over here already cut ...can I (unintelligible)...

03:59:29 Darin Routier ...(unintelligible) phone is right there...

04:01:28 Darlie Routier ...(unintelligible)...

04:03:01 RADIO...(unintelligible)...

04:05:02 Darlie Routier ...ya'll look out in the garage ...look out in the garage ...they left a knife laying on...

04:08:21 RADIO ...(unintelligible)...

04:09:19 911 Operator #1 ...there's a knife ...don't touch anything...

04:11:18 Darlie Routier ...I already touched it and picked it up...

04:12:05 RADIO ...10-4...

04:15:20 911 Operator #1 ...who's out there ...is anybody out there...

04:16:07 Police Officer ...(unintelligible)...

04:17:06 Darlie Routier ...I don't know ...I was sleeping...

04:18:14 911 Operator #1 ...ok ma'am ...listen ...there's a police officer at your front door ...is

your front door unlocked...

04:22:11 RADIO ...(unintelligible)...

04:22:15 Darlie Routier ...yes ma'am ...but where's the ambulance...

04:24:21 911 Operator #1 ...ok...

04:24:23 Darlie Routier ...they're barely breathing...

04:26:17 Darlie Routier ...if they don't get it here they're gonna be dead ...my God they're

(unintelligible) ...hurry ...please hurry...

04:31:13 911 Operator #1 ...ok ...they're ...they're...

04:32:18 Police Officer ...what about you...

04:33:06 911 Operator #1 ...is 82 out on Eagle...

04:34:18 Darlie Routier ...huh...

04:35:12 Darin Routier ...they took (unintelligible) ...they ran (unintelligible)...

04:36:28 911 Operator #2 ...(unintelligible)...

04:37:08 Darlie Routier ...we're at Eagle ...5801 Eagle ...my God and hurry...

04:41:03 RADIO ...(unintelligible)...

04:41:22 911 Operator #1 ...82 ...are you out...

04:42:25 Police Officer ...nothing's gone Mrs. Routier...

04:44:10 Darlie Routier ...oh my God ...oh my God ...why would they do this...

04:48:03 RADIO ...(unintelligible) to advise (unintelligible) 200...

04:50:18 Police Officer ...(unintelligible) the problem Mrs. Routier...

04:50:21 911 Operator #1 ...what'd he say..

04:51:29 Darlie Routier ...why would they do this...

04:53:08 Darlie Routier ...I'm (unintelligible)...

04:54:07 911 Operator #1 ...ok ...listen ma'am ...need to ...need to let the officers in the front

door ...ok...

04:59:11 Darlie Routier ...what...

05:00:04 911 Operator #1 ...ma'am..

05:00:22 Darlie Routier ...what ...what...

05:01:15 911 Operator #1 ...need to let the police officers in the front door...

05:04:21 Darlie Routier ...(unintelligible) his knife was lying over there and I already picked it up...

05:08:19 911 Operator #1 ...ok ...it's alright ...it's ok...

05:09:20 Darlie Routier ...God ...I bet if we could have gotten the prints maybe ...maybe...

05:13:18 Police Officer ...(unintelligible)...

05:14:18 RADIO ...82 ...we'll be (unintelligible)...

05:17:12 Darlie Routier ...ok ...it'll be...

05:18:08 911 Operator #1 ...ma'am ...hang on ...hang on a second...

05:19:09 Darlie Routier ...somebody who did it intentionally walked in here and did it Darin...

05:20:19 911 Operator #1 ...82 ...10-9...

05:21:23 RADIO ...(unintelligible)...

05:22:28 911 Operator #1 ...received...

05:23:05 Darlie Routier ...there's nothing touched...

05:24:12 911 Operator #1 ...ok ma'am...

05:25:13 Darlie Routier ...there's nothing touched...

05:26:20 RADIO ...(unintelligible)...

05:28:00 Darlie Routier ...oh my God...

05:29:08 Police Officer ...(unintelligible)...

05:29:23 RADIO ...received...

05:31:19 RADIO ...(unintelligible)...

05:33:25 911 Operator #1 ...ma'am ...is the police officer there...

05:35:14 Darlie Routier...yes (unintelligible)...

05:35:23 911 Operator #1 ...ok ...go talk to him ...ok...

05:38:03 RADIO ...(unintelligible)...

Total length of tape is 5:44:28

It was policeman David Waddell who arrived on the scene. He sickened at the sight, reeling back from the overwhelming smell of blood. Breathing deeply to contain his senses, the officer quickly surveyed the two children one appeared dead, the other with but a hint of a pulse he instructed Darlie to lay towels across Damon, and apply pressure to his wounds. She ignored him. She continued to scream at the officer that the intruder might still be in the garage. She described her attacker as a man of medium-to-tall height, dressed entirely in black: T-shirt, jeans and baseball cap.

Waddell was soon joined by another policeman, Sergeant Matthew Walling, and by a paramedic team of Jack Kolbye and Brian Koschak. Like Waddell, they paused at the threshold of the scene, momentarily disarmed by the top-heavy staleness of death. The paramedics immediately realized that they couldn't handle this carnage alone two children dead or dying and an adult woman soaked in blood, a bloody rag pressed to her throat and radioed for backup.

# Futile Efforts

Aside, Waddell briefed his sergeant. Together, they followed a path of blood through the house, from the entertainment room to the attached garage, accessible through the kitchen and a small utility room out back. Throwing their beam into the darkness of the garage until they found the light switch, they moved forward, revolvers drawn. They encountered no stranger along the route. However, they noticed that the screen on a side window of the garage had been visibly slashed down its center.

Realizing the attacker might still be in the house, the policemen checked out every room upstairs and down, every nook, closet and cranny in the house. Pausing now to take in the state of the kitchen, through which the killer was said to flee, noted its disarray its tiled floor spattered by blood; a vacuum cleaner knocked over as if in tumult, and, most ominous, a bloodied butcher knife resting silent now atop the island countertop. Beside the blade curiously lay a woman's latched purse and a set of women's expensive-looking jewelry, strangely untouched.

Upstairs they came across a third child, an infant, whimpering in its crib. Gently lifting the baby boy, Sgt. Walling examined him for bruises, but found none. Darin Routier, who met them below the steps, explained the child was their youngest, Drake, six months old.

The pair of paramedics had, in the meantime, been joined by three others Larry Byford, Eric Zimmerman and Rick Coleman. It had already become terribly clear that Damon was still alive, albeit barely, but that his brother Devon had died; the latter's eyes stared lifeless to the ceiling. Coleman had hastily assembled an IV tube to hopefully sustain the dying until they reached the hospital.

Assessing both boys' wounds, the medics noted two particularly large gashes, identifiably knife thrusts, in each of their chests. The thrusts had penetrated the children's lungs. Devon had died gasping, a horrible death. Damon's lungs, too, strained for oxygen, undeniably suffering the same fate that had claimed his sibling. Kolbye scooped Damon in his arms and maneuvered to the stretcher. He thought he heard the boy's death rattle, sounding as though his lungs expelled what little air they contained.

With the assistance of Coleman, Kolbye performed chest compressions to keep the boy alive. Wheeling him to the curb side ambulance, he simultaneously sluiced air to the trachea that the boy might receive precious air. The medics continued offering life-saving maneuvers the entire way to Baylor Medical Center across town, but the child died before they reached it.

# The Intruder

In the meantime, the K-9 unit had arrived on Eagle Drive, its animals unmuzzled and sent sniffing. Officer Waddell briefed its commander on the case and joined the team for a search of the neighborhood roundabout. This, while Sgt. Walling managed to calm the frantic Mrs. Routier on the front porch. While they gauzed her bleeding, she told the sergeant what she had told Waddell earlier: that an intruder had entered her home and mounted her on the sofa while she slept; she had awakened to him, screamed, and, after struggling with him, warding off his blows, he absconded toward the garage. It was then she noticed that he had left behind her two butchered boys. Of his attack on them, she had heard nothing.

She halted and grimaced as paramedics Koschak and Byford applied an IV line into her arm, then paused again as they placed Steri-Strips across a shallow but ugly throat cut. Recuperating from the smarting applications, she continued to speak to the policeman. She described her attacker as a man of medium-to-tall height, dressed entirely in black: T-shirt, jeans and baseball cap.

Three o'clock a.m., and Welling had concluded his interview. He stepped aside as the paramedics escorted her to their ambulance. She required further medical aid at Baylor Center. Darin told her he would follow; much too shaken to drive; he called on neighbor Tom Neal to drive him. Neal's wife remained behind to baby-sit infant Drake.

The Routiers were on their way to the hospital, but the police remained at their premises. In fact, their ranks grew in number. Squads drew up as an army, their rolling flashers severing the darkness to rudely lighten the cul-de-sac where the Routiers lived. Neighbors, roused from their beds, emerged from their dark homes to their assorted yards to gape as troops of dark uniforms flanked in marching fashion around and through the Routier house, across its lawn, through its colonial-style front door. Under the glare of the torch, police threw up a cordon around the property. The staring citizens had never expected to see anything like this in Rowlett, here in the crime-free suburb of Dalrock Heights Addition. Especially on their own street.

# Suspicions

Because of its severity, the crime scene drew Rowlett's law enforcement honchos. Among them was Lieutenant Grant Jack, commander of the Investigative Division. Summoned from his bed, he arrived shortly after 3 a.m. and viewed the battle-hardened appearance of Eagle Drive.

In the foyer of 5801, he met Detective Jimmy Patterson, a veteran of the Crimes Against Persons Division, who pointed out the Routier child, Devon, still lying under a blanket. He explained what he knew up to this time concerning the slayings that the mother claimed a stranger had committed the atrocities and a butcher knife (murder weapon) lay where the police found it, on the kitchenette counter, bloodied. The mother, said Patterson, had put it there after lifting it off the floor after the killer dropped it.

As the two professionals conferred, their forces uniformed and in plain clothes steam-rolled throughout the home's many rooms looking for suspicious objects and possible clues. Ascending the Routier's circular staircase to the second floor, a couple of them were accosted by a yapping white Pomeranian that rounded the upper landing to hold them at bay; the animal nipped Patrolman Mark Wyman's trouser leg. Karen Neal, on hand, rushed to the rescue.

"It's Karen, Domain, Karen! Now leave the policemen alone and get in your corner!" she scolded. Corralling Domain, she apologized to the police and explained that the dog was averse to strangers. The patrolmen, and probably Karen Neal too, wondered where this watchdog had been during the all-important time of break-in. He might have saved two lives.

Lieutenant Jack, a professional in the law enforcement field for more than 20 years, had never witnessed slaughter like this in such a peaceful, suburban community; it left him pondering the creature that caused this, that walked on two feet and called itself human. And when the morgue attendants zipped what was left of little Devon into the standard black plastic body bag, the officer, who considered himself a pretty tough person, turned his face away to bawl like a baby.

"For months, when I'd came home from work, I'd walk into my five-year-old's room to check on him," Jack later recalled. "When I looked at my son sleeping, I didn't see him, I saw Damon in the morgue and Devon on the floor...I just couldn't shake the vision."

But, it wasn't just the physicality that gnawed at Jack. It was something else. Something deep under that warned his psyche: *Something doesn't add up here.* Patterson felt it, too, and admitted it. A strong sense of the macabre crept into their bones.

Jack put Patterson and his partner, Chris Frosch, in charge of the investigation; he sent Frosch to the hospital, in fact, to interview Mrs. Routier at first chance. He needed to get as much *detailed* information as he could about what happened in this house to cause such blood-letting and havoc. So far, too many blanks existed. And too many suspicions, Maybe wayward, maybe premature.

Eagle Drive had become a rush. Media crews had assembled and cameras flashed in the darkness, catching police activity. The whiteness of their spotlights illumined the pre-dawn hours and mingled with the colors of the squads' rotating "cherry" beams to stroke a bizarre texture of light across the dark canvas somewhat, Jack thought, like the thread-thin line between nightmare and awakening. The lieutenant squinted into the light of the overheads and shook his head at the attention these tragedies always attract.

Away from the ears of the cameramen, Sgt. Walling drew his superior into his confidence; he looked stunned. "Lieutenant, you won't believe what Mr. Routier said to me right before he left to go to the hospital with his wife. He turned to me and I swear to God he said, 'Golly, I guess this is the biggest thing Rowlett's ever had.' The man had two of his children slaughtered tonight, and he's acting like the damn circus is in town!"

No, Jack thought to himself, things didn't add up.

# The Crime scene

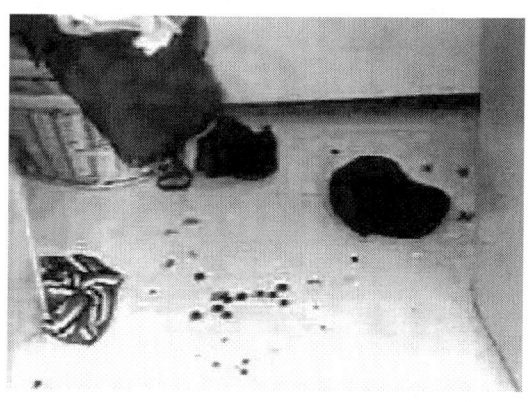

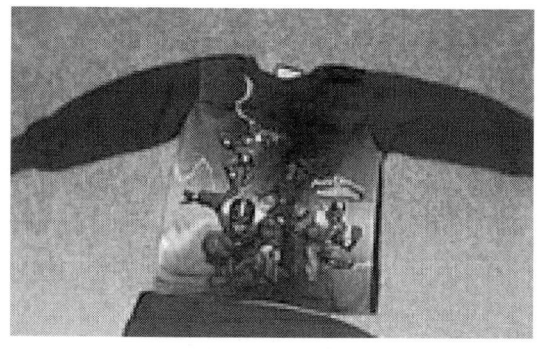

Devon's Power Rangers pajamas

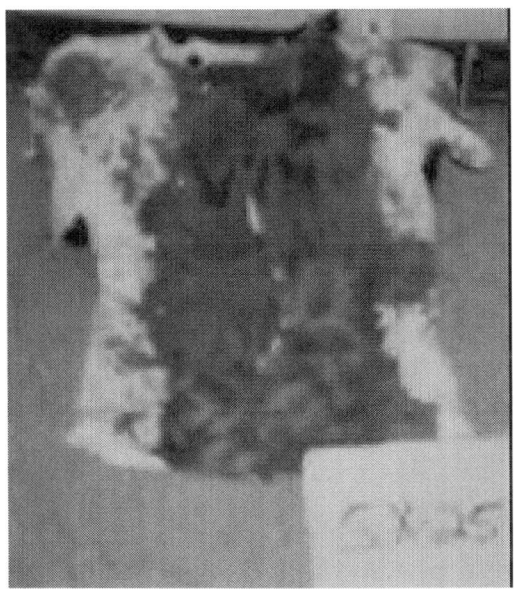

Darlie's nightshirt

Location of the sock containing bloodstains

# The murder weapon

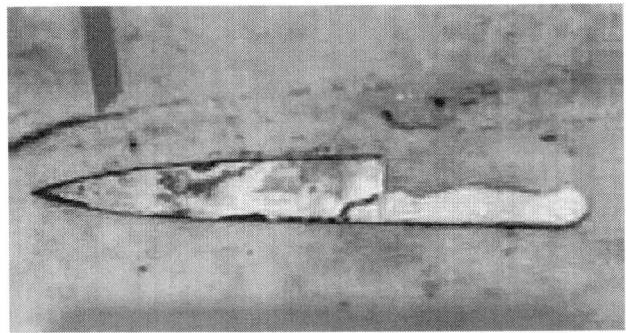

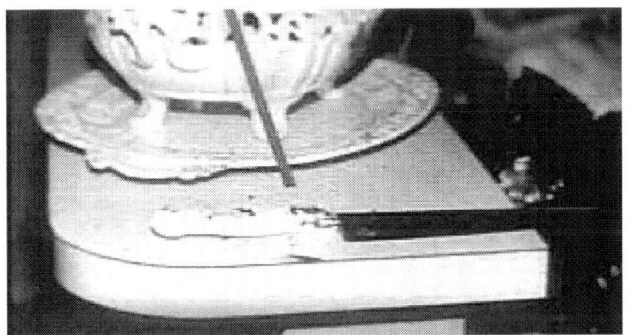

The Routier home buzzed with stark-faced policemen taking stark notes, shooting stark crime photos, dusting for fingerprints that would tell a stark tale. In the kitchenette, something very telling had occurred. Sgt. Nabors thought it was strange that the sink was spotless and white while the floors and edges of the countertop around and above it were blood-smudged. And if someone had taken the effort to clean the sink of blood *why*? His job being to process blood traces at a crime scene, Nabors went to work.

"(He) conducted a test to detect the presence of human blood that cannot be seen with the naked eye," explains the book, *Precious Angels*. "The chemical compound Luminol is the tool that investigators use for this test. If the white crystalline compound in the Luminol detects the copper component found in human blood, the area sprayed becomes luminescent, casting a brilliant bluish light. The sergeant sprayed the sink and the surrounding counter. When the lights were switched off, the entire sink basin and the surrounding counter glowed in the dark."

Repeating this process on the leatherette sofa, the detective found a small child's handprint glowing iridescent blue near the edge where Damon had been stabbed. Like the blood in the kitchen, someone had wiped it away. Again *why*?

Simultaneously to Nabors' findings, crime scene consultant James Cron found other variables of the case out of sync. Like Sgt. Nabors, he realized what appeared to be *wasn't*. The moment he arrived at 5801 Eagle Drive, his years of experience told him, as he began taking mental notes that Darlie Routier's testimony of what happened *didn't*.

The questionable point of entry, the garage screen

Mrs. Routier had stated she believed the killer had gotten in and escaped through the garage. Indeed, Cron found, as the woman said, a slit screen on the side of the house, in the garage but he knew at first glance it was a no-go. The screen showed no signs of having been forcibly pushed in or out to allow a body through its netting, but even more telling was the fact that the screen's frame was easily removable. Any criminal with an idiot's IQ would have simply taken it off its setting. Additionally, the ground below the window, comprised of a dewy, wet mulch, was undisturbed. Perhaps, he figured, the woman in her panicked condition may have been wrong perhaps the intruder had found other ingress and egress so he rounded the entire home for other visible indications of breaking and entry. He found none.

# Crime Scene Tells Story

Returning inside, he followed the bloody footprints. They indeed led from the room where the children were slain through to a utility room then onto the concrete floor of the garage, trailing off below its window. But, again, the screen seemed an unlikely escape port. Doubling that suspicion, the dust on the sill was undisturbed, there were no hand prints, bloody or otherwise, around the window; odd, since the killer in forcing his way through the window would have had to hang onto the walls for balance!

The investigator double-tracked to the yard, this time looking for drops of blood left behind by the slayer in flight. Surely, his savagery had produced vast amounts of blood and his clothing would have been dripping with it yet there were no apparent traces beyond the interior of the house. Not on the mulch below the window, not on the yard's manicured lawn, not along nor atop the six-foot high fence that surrounded the yard, not in the alley. *The blood was contained within the house. Nowhere else.*

In the entertainment room where Darlie described a struggle, Cron found little evidence of a melee having taken place. The lampshade was askew, and an expensive flower arrangement lay beside the coffee table. Nothing more out of place. He found, in fact, the fragile stems of the flowers unbroken as if the arrangement hadn't fallen, but been placed there.

In the kitchenette, only Darlie's bloodied footprints were visible. Pieces of a shattered wineglass, too, lay among the prints, and a vacuum cleaner had been deposited on its side. Blood underneath these items indicated, to him, that they were dropped after not before, nor during the violence.

Atop the kitchen counter sat Darlie's purse, which appeared in order and undisturbed, and several pieces of jewelry rings, a bracelet and a watch aligned in order, untouched.

Reports author Barbara Davis in *Precious Angels*: "Everything the professional saw at the crime scene disturbed him. The lack of a blood trail away from the home coupled with virtually no signs of a struggle bothered him most."

Late afternoon, after his thorough and all-day examination, he summarized his findings for Lt. Jack and Sgt. Walling. "We all know the crime scene tells the story. Problem is," he nodded, "that story's not the same one the mother's telling. Somebody inside this house did this thing. Gentlemen, there was no intruder."

# The Trauma Room

Months later, in court, the prosecution would attempt to demonstrate Darlie Routier as a heartless, cold-blooded killer. Much of their testimony came from the staff of Baylor Medical Center, where the dead boys were delivered and where Darlie Routier was admitted for observation. Almost immediately, the hospital's personnel sensed something amiss with the mother, for while she outwardly seemed agitated by her tragedy, repeating over and over "Who could have done this to my boys?" her reaction struck them as insincere and artificial.

Trauma nurse Jody Fitts, an RN for eight years, recalls, "Darlie was wheeled by Trauma Room 1, where her dead child was. She glanced over there, and I was very concerned she would get more upset. His physical condition alone was disconcerting. He was nude and covered head to toe in blood. Tubes were still held in place with tape, and brown bags had been placed around his little-bitty hands to preserve any possible evidence. It was a very stressful and horrible sight...I'll never forget it. (Darlie) saw him. She had absolutely no response, just turned her head back and stared straight ahead cold as ice."

# Darlie's wounds

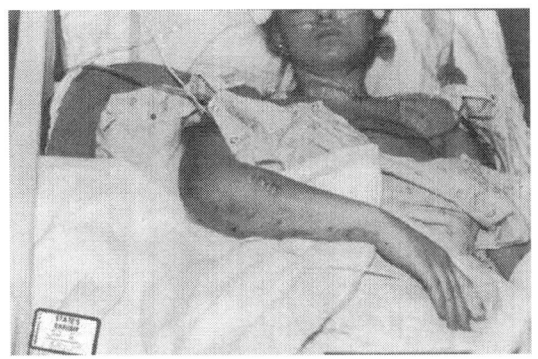

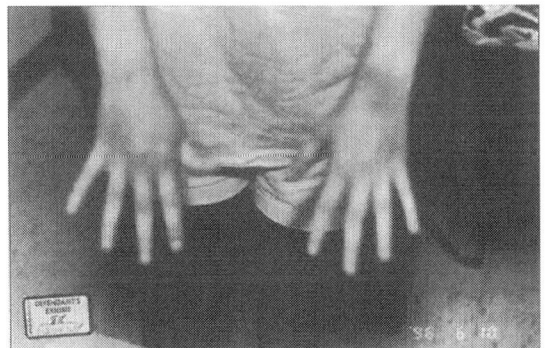

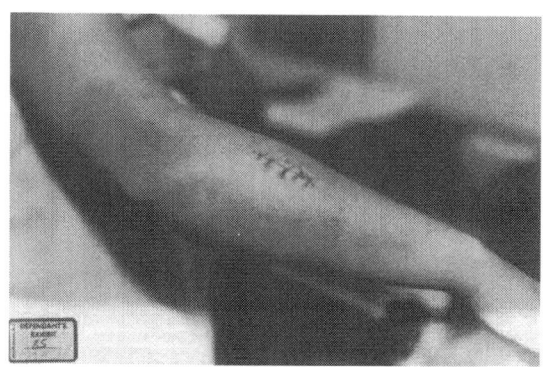

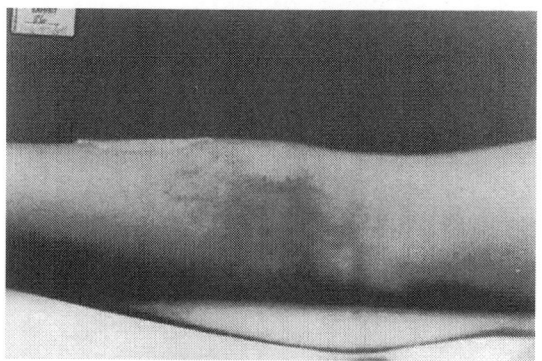

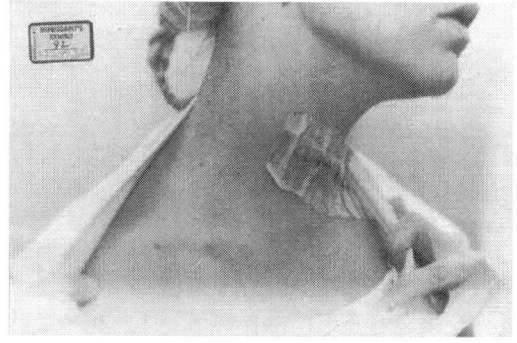

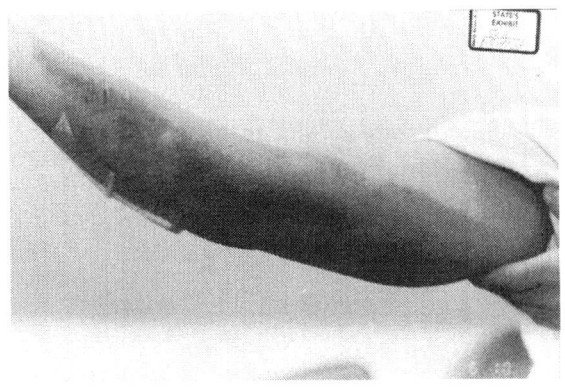

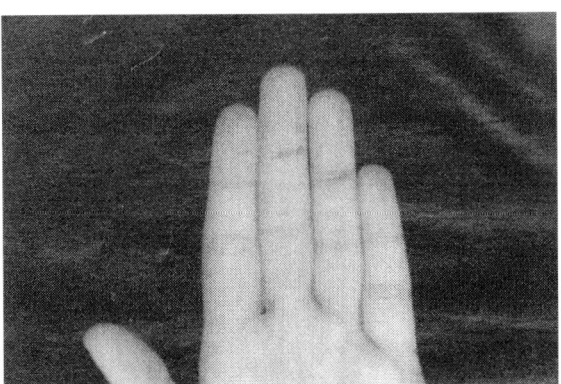

Checking the woman's condition, examining doctors Santos and Dillawn found the mother's wounds superficial. Under the scratches and blood, they uncovered some minor cuts, which they stitched, and a gash on the throat. While the later left a sickening sight, it was not dangerous, they asserted. The platysma, a sheath protecting the jugular vein, was uncut. Santos, nevertheless, made the decision to keep her in check for several days, considering the strain of the ordeal she suffered. She was berthed in the Intensive Care Unit (ICU) under supervision and hooked up to the procedural heart monitor, IV and oxygen tank.

# Indifference

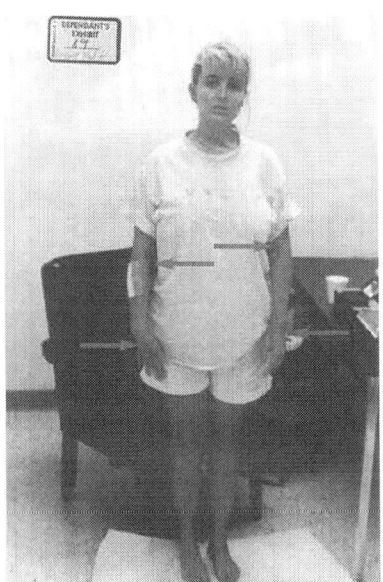

Darlie Routier

On Thursday, the day after the murders, Darlie was again interviewed by the police, this time by detectives Jimmy Patterson and Chris Frosch. She reiterated her story of the attack. Her description was slightly more detailed than before:

"I woke up hearing my son Damon saying 'Mommy Mommy,' as he tugged on my nightshirt. I opened my eyes and felt a man get off me. I got up to chase after him. As I flipped the light in the kitchen on, I saw him open his hand and let the knife drop to the floor. Then he ran out through the garage. I went over and picked up the knife. I shouldn't have picked it up. I probably covered up the fingerprints. I shouldn't have picked it up.

"I looked over and saw my two babies with blood all over them. I didn't realize my own throat had been cut until I saw myself in a mirror. I screamed out to my husband."

Male nurse Christopher Wielgosz was on hand during the interview. He noted how she continuously seemed to admonish herself even to other hospital personnel before and after the interview for picking up the murder weapon and erasing the intruder's fingerprints. It seemed as if she wanted the point driven home why her finger prints were on that knife.

Various other staff members who attended to Darlie throughout her short stay at Baylor complained that she seemed far removed from despair, even cold to the situation. Nurse Jody Cotner describes the scene she saw while Darlie's family visited after she was admitted to the ICU: "Her mother, Darlie Kee, and her little sister, God bless their hearts ...they were hysterical. I probably held her sister I don't know how long. They were all sobbing. All except Darlie."

Cotner, who has worked with trauma patients for more than a decade, adds, "The reaction of people who lose their children is a wide range of emotions, bur mothers are always inconsolable (but) in my entire nursing experience I have never seen a reaction like Darlie's."

Paige Campbell's remarks echo Cotner's. Says Nurse Campbell, "People react differently, but there is a commonality when someone...sees someone they love die. But I had never seen a reaction like Darlie's before. There were tissues by the bed, but she never took one."

Denise Faulk, a nurse who attended to Darlie during her first night in the ICU was so bothered by Darlie's nonchalance that she went home after her tour of duty and recorded her observations of the woman's behavior. Responsible for washing the blood off Darlie's feet, she had expected the woman to break down. But, she noted, the mother had displayed complete indifference.

Dr. Santos released his patient on Saturday morning so she could attend her sons' wake that evening at Rest Haven Funeral Home. Detectives Patterson and Frosch, however, first escorted Darlie and her husband Darin to the station house for statements. Procedurally given the Miranda Rights, Darlie wrote her official statement, which recalled the events of the preceding Wednesday morning. In this version she penned that she was awakened by Damon *who was still standing on his feet* when he uttered 'Mommy Mommy'.

In the anteroom, Patterson explained to Lt. Jack something he had caught in his last conversation with Mrs. Routier while she was still bedridden. When he had mentioned to her that her dog Domain had tried to bite a patrolman, she fleetingly remarked, "Oh, he always goes off like that when someone he doesn't know walks in the door." Jack gave him a *I hope you made a note of that* expression, in return.

# I'm Sorry

Family, friends and neighbors turned out that Saturday evening at the funeral parlor. The boys were suited in tiny tuxedos in separate walnut caskets, enveloped by roses of red and white. Upon entering the chapel, Darlie knelt at their sides and whispered to them (Detective Frosch overheard), "I'm sorry." She then wailed, "Who could have done this to my children?"

After Darin calmed her down, mourners strode forward to express their condolences. One mourner, Helina Czaban, who sometimes performed general housekeeping duties for the Routiers, was thrown off balance by her employer's remarks.

When she told Darlie how sorry she was for the tragedy, adding, "...and now this expensive funeral to add to your problems," Darlie replied, "I'm not worried. I'll get five-thousand dollars each for both of the boys."

During the hour-long service the next day, "she didn't wipe her eyes," exclaimed a relative, "never cried...There is no mistaking grief."

As the families tried to comfort Darin, Darlie busied herself by looking at the names on the flower arrangements and comforting her relatives...The family would try to excuse Darlie's lack of emotion by blaming the pills (Xanax) the doctor had prescribed. As the family wept before the boys' coffins, Darlie made the comment that she had to be sure to send thank-you notes to all who sent flowers.

# Of Shadows and Silly String

Darlie Routier had not yet returned to her home on Eagle Drive since that horrible morning; she, Darin and baby Drake had been staying with Mama Darlie in Plano. Needing some articles of clothing, she telephoned her friend Mercedes Adams a few days after the funeral to ask if she would mind driving her there. Mercedes complied, but expected Darlie to buckle under upon walking into the place that took the lives of her two sons. The girlfriend was in for an awakening.

Death lingered in the foyer, but Darlie, Mercedes noted, charged onto the scene seemingly unaware and like a bull elephant, arms akimbo, shouted, "Look at this mess! It'll cost us a fortune to fix this shit!"

"Right there where her boys were killed, and that's the first thing she said to me. I put my hands on Darlie's shoulders and said, 'Darlie, look me in the eye and tell me you didn't kill the boys.' She looked me in the eye and said, 'I'm gonna get new carpet, new drapes, and fix this room all up.' I couldn't believe it."

Back at the Rowlett Police Station, questions loomed. Among them:

1) What was the motive for the murders?

2) If a robbery, why was Darlie's jewelry and purse left untouched?

3) Why would an intruder kill two children before killing the adult, who posed a more serious threat?

4) Why would the killer, who obviously had no scruples about murdering a pair of small boys, back off when Darlie awoke, leaving a witness alive to identify him?

5) Why would he drop the murder weapon on the floor, giving Darlie, his pursuer, a weapon in which to fight back?

6) Why would he have used the Routiers' butcher knife in the first place? (Assailants come to their intended victim's premises already armed.)

7) Why were there no visible signs of an intruder footprints, handprints, drops of blood beyond the house where he made his escape? And as questions mounted, it appeared that a bread knife owned by the Routiers might have been used to cut the garage screen, thus more questions:

8) Had the intruder used the Routier's bread knife to slash his way in?

9) If so, how did he get the knife in the first place?

Detective Jimmy Patterson conferred with Dr. Townsend-Parchman, who had photographed Darlie's wounds allegedly received by the phantom intruder. While her boys were maliciously and forcefully attacked, her wounds were surface and bore trademarks of what doctors call "hesitation wounds" that is, the wounds indicated that the blade had slowly, deliberately, cut into her skin and, when pain was encountered, the person holding the blade reflexively withdrew it.

Rowlett police had turned to the FBI's Center for Analysis of Violent Crime in Quantico, Virginia, to evaluate and compare the wounds of the dead boys to those of Darlie. The FBI's Al Brantley, after studying the doctors' and coroner's reports as well as the crime findings in general attested that the wounds between sons and mother were indeed vastly different Darlie's superficial, Damon's and Devon's massive and mortal. The attack on the children was personal, said Brantley. "The killer focused on their chests," he emphasized, "almost as if going for their heart. That indicates extreme anger toward them."

Brantley reported other observations. "For a violent struggle to take place as the mother claimed, no real breakage occurred. After looking at the crime-scene photographs, it appeared to me that the intruder who committed this crime had a strong connection to the material items in the home. The living room was fairly small and compressed. Two adults fighting would have resulted in a lot more broken things. A lot of fragile items in the living room that should have taken the brunt of a struggle were not broken."

His conclusion: Damon's and Devon's slayer was someone who knew them and knew the premises. The entire scenario had been planned in advance and staged.

# The Graveside Party

The most bizarre of post-murder episodes was yet to take place in what became the state's case against Darlie Lynn Routier. It was a birthday party eerily held graveside to celebrate Devon's seventh birthday posthumously!

Darlie and Darin Routier, infant Drake, Darlie's mother, 16-year-old-sister Dana who still lived at home with the elder Mama Darlie and a few invited personal friends were the celebrants. Local television station KXAS-TV was on hand to record the strange event. Darlie told Joe Munoz, a reporter, that the family had planned a whopping birthday prior to her son's death and that she saw no reason now why he should have it deprived. To many of the NBC media crew on hand at Rest Haven Memorial Park that morning of June 14, it seemed like one of three things: either a bad PR attempt of Darlie's, a sincere but naïve show of goodwill done in poor taste...or simple, plain, unmitigated lunacy.

Neither the Routiers nor the TV crew was aware that Jimmy Patterson's investigators were recording the party from a concealed camcorder, a microphone also having been planted nearby to catch any possible confessional remark.

A pastor opened the 45-minute ceremony over the grave, yet unmarked by a headstone. His sincere attempts to sanctify the moment, however, were overshadowed by what happened when he finished his eulogy. As horrified home viewers watched, Darlie began spraying a can of Silly String across the newly padded ground, laughing, chewing bubble gum and singing Happy Birthday. "I love you, Devon and Damon!" she cried.

To justify her actions, she afterward told Munoz, "If you knew (my sons), you'd know that they are up there in heaven having the biggest birthday party we could ever imagine. And though our hearts are breaking, they wouldn't want us to be unhappy. But they'll be a part of us always."

Responding to questions about her boys' mystery killer, she said, "The only thing that keeps me going is the hope that they will find that person. I have faith in God. I believe He will direct the police to that man."

Four days after the birthday party, on January 18, the Rowlett Police Department arrested Darlie Routier for the murder of her two children.

# Preparing the Trial

Americans had been horrified at the destruction of two little boys' lives and now, with news that their mother might be their murderer, they were stunned.

Darlie remained under custody at the Lew Starrett Justice Center, awaiting indictment. A Dallas County grand jury officially indicted her on June 28, on two counts of capital murder. That same day, Judge Mark Tolle, who would preside at her trial, issued a gag warrant that barred both the defense and prosecution from discussing the case with the media. This, of course, eliminated any of the direct players' participation on TV talk and radio shows.

Doug Parks with Darlie in court

Doug Parks, Darlie's court-appointed lawyer, presented a request to Judge Tolle on July 9, recommending that the trial be moved out of Dallas County where he claimed bad publicity would prejudice jury members. The motion went into consideration and before the trial would open on its scheduled date in January, 1997, it would indeed be moved to the town of Kerrville in neighboring Bexar County.

Parks' move was well orchestrated since, four days after; State Prosecutor Greg Davis announced in dramatic fashion that he would seek the death penalty.

While such seemed unlikely the last woman to be executed in Texas was during the Civil War young but brilliant Davis had a knack for getting what he went after. Assisting him would be two rising prosecution attorneys, Sherri Wallace and Toby Shook.

Immediately after her incarceration, Darlie had demanded that she be given a polygraph test, which the police agreed to administer. When she was informed that her husband Darin could not be present in the room during the test, she withdrew her request. However, she again changed her mind on advice from her defense team, but with a stipulation: that before she takes the polygraph she exercise her right to take a private test first.

The results of that test were never formally released, but Darlie and her mother were seen immediately afterwards, sobbing relentlessly.

After the prosecution announced its death pursuit, the Routier in-laws hurriedly dropped the state-supplied lawyer assigned to Darlie and, knowing they needed big guns to fight back, mortgaged their homes to procure the services of headline defense attorney, Doug Mulder, late of the district attorney's office. To counteract the legal backup talent pressed against his client, he assembled a grade-A team, which included a retired FBI investigator.

Jury selection began October 16, 1996 in Kerrville. The process would take two days short of a month. Because of the media frenzy *is Darlie guilty or isn't she?* Unfounded truths and rumors were flying amidst the tabloids and even major newspapers; lawyers from both sides wanted to ensure they had selected a jury worthy of the impartiality that a body of jurors was supposed to comprise. On November 14, they announced the voi dire complete: seven women and five men would be the final deciders of Darlie Routier's case after what promised to be a trial of high suspense.

Darin Routier, Mama Darlie and other family supporters took lodging in local hotels, where they would remain near the accused throughout the trial. Over his head in bills, Darin had by this time deserted the now-dreaded family home in Dalrock Heights Addition, transferring all personal possessions into storage. He let the mortgage payments lapse and, in mid-December, the mortgage company repossessed the property, six months *in arrears*.

It was claimed that at the time of foreclosure, the only reminder of the Routiers' lives there was a pair of little boys' gym shoes, left abandoned on the front porch.

# The Trial Begins

Darlie Routier being transported to court

Eyes and ears of the world were on Kerrville, Texas. Attests Barbara Davis' *Precious Angels*: "On Monday morning (January 6, 1997) crowds descended on the stately but tiny courthouse, buffeted by fierce winter winds...Visitors to the courthouse were subjected to rigorous security. Each had to pass through a metal-detector gate and hand over purses and briefcases to be searched...No newspapers, cameras or tape recorders were allowed."

The district attorney's office, being relentless, had decided to concentrate its initial armament against Darlie on the death of only one of her boys, Damon. Holding the capital murder indictment on Devon's death in limbo, they could use it as second-line support should the woman be acquitted or receive a life sentence.

When the indictment was recited first degree murder in the death of Damon Christian Routier Darlie stood facing the judge. Shouldered by her lawyer, Doug Mulder, she pleaded Not Guilty.

Curtain up on the long-awaited trial.

Darlie stands to answer Not Guilty in court

Chief Prosecutor Greg Davis' opening remarks thundered, "The evidence will show you, ladies and gentlemen, that Darlie Routier is a self-centered, materialistic woman cold enough to murder two precious children..." He vowed to prove how the facts of the case as found by experts did not match the mother's explanation of what happened in her home the night of the brutal killings.

Defense Attorney Mulder, in turn, painted Darlie as a caring mother who, like any other housewife, suffered personal problems and concerns. She was, he said, caught up in a maelstrom of fate. "And the State wants you to believe she became a psychotic killer in the blink of an eye?" he asked. "Well, folks, that's just absurd!"

# The Prosecution

The trial would last nearly a month. Proceedings began with the introduction of the first witness for the State, Dr. Joanie McLaine from the medical examiner's office. Dr. McLaine explained the two defense wounds on Damon's body, indicating that he had struggled with his attacker before dying.

Coroner Janice Townsend-Parchman described the differences between the children's' savage wounds and Darlie's hesitation wounds, suggesting Darlie inflicted her wounds on herself.

Officer Waddell, the first policeman on the scene the morning of June 6, testified to the carnage that confronted him inside the Routier house when he entered. Jury members were shown crime scene photographs, which detailed the aftermath of the violence.

Following this dramatic play, paramedic Jack Kolbye related heart-tugging testimony of tending to little Damon and watching, despite any given life-saving measurements, the boy's final struggle for air through bloody, slashed lungs.

The first week's witness presentations ended on a very negative note for Darlie Lynn Routier. Following Kolbye's vivid story, fellow paramedic Larry Byford, who examined her in the ambulance on the way to the hospital, claimed that during the entire trip she didn't ask once about the condition of her children.

# The Nurses

A litany of medical personnel were called to testify at the trial. The prosecution called nurses and doctors who treated Darlie at the Baylor Medical Center to testify about their experiences with her. The testimony provided at trial was contradictory to the notes recorded in Darlie's medical records during her hospital stay. This page examines the contradictions that were presented in court. It is also important to note that several nurses who attended to Darlie during her stay were not called by the prosecution to testify.

On the 6th of June, medical notes indicate that Darlie's family was at her bedside continuously. One note reads: "Encouraged family members to allow pt. to rest + avoid talking to pt. or mentioning the assault".

Various notations also indicated that she was regularly receiving pain medication (and sometimes anxiety medication). She was under the influence of this medication when questioned by police. She repeatedly maintained her home was broken into and that an intruder attacker her and her children.

## Dr. Patrick Dillawn

On June 6 of 1996, Doctor Dillawn was working when Darlie was brought into the emergency department. He testified about her injuries, the surgery performed on her neck and her demeanor during the time he interacted with her.

Prosecutor Toby Shook questioned him and asked about his experience with shock and trauma. He asked Dr. Dillawn to describe Darlie's emotional state and he said that she seemed agitated about the police being there and photographing her. He went on to say, "She did not seem particularly upset other than that".

Shook asked the doctor if he saw tears streaming down Darlie's face and he answered, "At the end of my visit she did cry a little bit. She had a photograph of her children in her hand. And then she cried a little bit".

However, that was not what the doctor recorded in his notes. In the report below, that he wrote and signed, Dr. Dillawn described Darlie as "tearful" and "frightened".

Dr. Dillawn's report

The doctor was asked on cross-examination if he read through the notes made by the nurses who attended to Darlie, over the course of her stay at the hospital, and he stated that he had not.

He was asked if he would be surprised to learn that over the course of her three-day stay various nurses described her as tearful, frightened, and upset. He responded by saying, "No, it would not surprise me."

Indeed it shouldn't have since that is exactly what the nurses recorded throughout their notes, contrary to statements later made on the stand.

**Jody Fitts**

Fitts was a registered nurse at Baylor Medical Center in June of 1996 when Darlie was transported to the hospital and underwent surgery pertaining to her neck injury. Fitts testified he was on duty during the early morning hours when Darlie was admitted.

Under direct examination the nurse testified that when Darlie was first brought into the emergency department she was hysterical and screaming. Fitts observed her asking why someone would kill her boys. Her clothes had been completely removed and Fitts said she was "covered head to toe in dried blood".

He described Darlie's wounds – including her neck wound which spurted blood when touched by one of the surgeons. He also mentioned the necklace that was embedded in the wound and "freed" when the nurse removed the bandage the paramedics had applied. His testimony implied the necklace was not embedded in the wound, but if it had been loose around Darlie's neck it would have been removed, along with all her other clothing while she was initially treated.

The necklace is contained in an evidence room in Dallas, Texas. Nicks made by the knife that cut Darlie's throat are visible in the chain in two spots. Below are pictures of each.

First nick in necklace

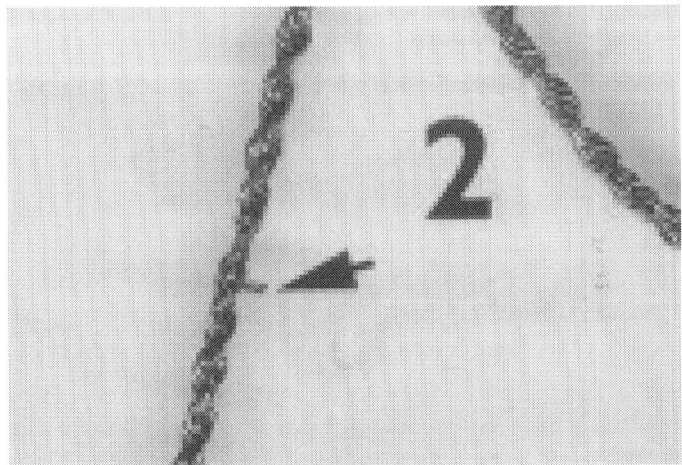

Second nick in necklace

Fire department employee Byford testified that he observed the necklace on Darlie before she arrived at the hospital. He tried to remove it but it caused her pain and so he left it there.

Fitts testified that he removed the necklace and that it was "unattached", meaning he did not have to undo it.

He testified that Darlie was able to answer questions.

The defense did not cross examine Fitts.

## Christopher Wielgosz

Wielgosz worked as a nurse in the intensive care unit at Baylor University Medical Center. He was working when Darlie was brought to the ICU from the operating room where she had surgery on her neck earlier that morning.

Wielgosz testified that the first comment Darlie made in his presence was, "How could anyone do this to my children?" He did not ask her any questions about what had happened to her, but he was aware that she had been "involved in a trauma" and that two of her children had also been involved.

He stated that she repeated her question about how someone could do something like that to her children. Then he said that she mentioned the attacker dropping a knife and Darlie stating she had picked it up and was worried that she had "obscured the attacker's fingerprints".

Though the nurse stated that Darlie was alert and aware, he acknowledged that the comments she made were not consistent. "She wasn't speaking consistently," he testified and explained she would make those kinds of comments "periodically".

He testified that he gave her pain medication in the form of 25 milligrams of Demerol combined with a drug called

Phenergan. This medication was administered to her shortly before she was questioned by the police.

Wielgosz testified that while Darlie was in his care "she was — her eyes were tearful, but she had a very flat affect". It was a curious statement considering what he recorded in his notes about how she was "crying" and "visibly upset".

Wielgosz indicated under cross-examination that he had been called to the Rowlett Police Department to make a statement. He also stated that he had spoken to prosecutor Shook the day before he testified. The nurses called to testify stayed together prior to giving their testimony at the Holiday Inn. He acknowledged that they all sometimes ate together during that stay.

**Jody Cotner**

Jody Cotner was a trauma nurse at Baylor in June of 1996. She arrived at the hospital around 8 a.m. the morning Darlie was admitted. Her first encounter with her occurred while Darlie was in bed in the ICU.

Cotner recounted meeting Darlie, testifying that she introduced herself and then asked Darlie about what happened. She stated that Darlie told her about the attack and described chasing her attacker and picking up the knife. She then testified she met with Darlie periodically throughout the day.

She also downplayed Darlie's emotional state, suggesting that she was not grieving as a mother normally would. However, on cross-examination she testified that she had not taken any notes in reference to Darlie because she did "not do direct patient care in the intensive care unit". She did help to change and dress Darlie's injuries though.

The issue of the bruising came up during cross-examination and the nurse was resistant to admitting that it would be negligent for any of the nurses to fail to note bruising on Darlie while she was in the hospital. She also provided a vague range for which she believed bruising observed on one of the photographs presented as an exhibit could have been caused, suggesting a time frame that would have occurred while Darlie was still in the hospital. However, when challenged on this point she admitted that it was unlikely Darlie received that kind of blunt force trauma while under the care of the hospital. She also agreed there was a wide range of time in which the bruising could have occurred.

**Diane Hollon**

Hollon was another nurse at Baylor who testified at Darlie's trial. She described getting to the hospital at 6:45 a.m. She came into contact with Darlie around 8 a.m. She testified about Darlie's demeanor, saying that she "didn't show a whole lot of emotions". She did admit to charting that Darlie "would get tearful".

She stated that Darlie would touch her boys' pictures, become tearful, and make statements about how she could not believe her babies were gone. Hollon testified Darlie did this several times throughout the day that she was with her.

Hollon, like the other nurses, minimized Darlie's expression of emotion during her hospital stay. However, a prior nurse's brief notes regarding Darlie's demeanor, approximately a half hour before Hollon received her, reported Darlie was "very emotional" and had "periods of crying/sobbing".

It is unclear who made that particular notation. It does not appear to have been Wielgosz because he signed his notations with his initials and he also included the year in the date portion. The notation was made a half hour before Hollon received Darlie and so it was not likely her writing. Who was it? Why were they not called to testify? Whoever the person was indicated that Darlie became "very emotional" while "talking about events + family". If put on the stand, would they have contradicted the other nurses' testimony?

Hollon's notes were recorded on the sheet at 8:00 a.m.

Hollon tried to downplay Darlie's emotional state by claiming something that contradicted the previous nurse's notation, saying: "She never did actually burst out crying, sobbing, nothing like that".

She admitted to having met with the prosecutors on multiple occasions before she testified as well.

### Paige Campbell

Campbell testified on behalf of the prosecution as well. She claimed that Darlie was not emotional and that she never saw a tear run down Darlie's face. It was yet another odd claim since her notes indicated Darlie was "very tearful". She also stated in the notes that Darlie asked to have a family member in her room with her at all times, indicating her need for support and her fear of being alone after such a traumatic event. Campbell indicated emotional support was given to Darlie in response to her emotional state.

On the stand Campbell tried to trivialize Darlie's expression of emotion just as the other nurses had done. She never gave a plausible explanation about the contradiction between the notes and her testimony.

### Denise Faulk

Faulk was another nurse at Baylor. She came in contact with Darlie late in the evening of the 6th and attended to her until 7 a.m. the following morning. She testified that at one point Darlie described the attack, stating that she had wrestled with a man.

Faulk said that Darlie was not crying when she relayed the story and that she saw her eyes get wet, but "never really saw tears go down her face".

However, in her notes she wrote, "Pt. tearful @ times". She also noted that the family provided emotional support and that Darlie was encouraged to rest.

**Others Who Didn't Testify**

There were at least four nurses recorded throughout the notes who were not called to testify by the prosecutor. The defense did not call these nurses to the stand either. However, there was much the defense did not do that they should have such as conduct their own independent DNA testing and enter the prayer vigil video that took place before the silly string video – to name just two.

A chaplain attended to Darlie around 9:00 a.m. and recorded two notes on the page containing notations about her discharge. He appeared to have spent at least one hour with her because he made a second notation at 10:00 a.m. The name appears to read "Don Hicks" or "Don Hick". The prosecution never called him to testify about Darlie's lack of emotion and he noted that upon meeting with her she was "very upset".

A nurse by the name of V. McCright made notations about attending to Darlie on the 7th as well. The person reported that Darlie was "tearful".

Finally, a nurse with the last name of "Fisher" attended to Darlie the evening of the 7th and into the morning of the 8th. The person noted that a guard was posted outside until midnight and that when there was no one there, Darlie's husband Darin became upset.

Who were these people? If what they observed matched the other nurses' claims on the stand, why weren't they called to testify against Darlie as well? If they had testified that Darlie was emotional and grieving (as the various notes strongly suggest) would it have influenced the jury to acquit Darlie?

Over the next couple of weeks, verbal shrapnel continued to tear the accused apart, word by word, despite the defense's attempts for cover. Kicking off the second week of the prosecution's assault were two members of the Rowlett police force, Officer David Maynes, who discussed some of the evidence uncovered from the crime scene (including a section of white carpeting bearing Damon's bloodied handprint), and fingerprint expert Charles Hamilton, who, basically, told the jury that the only prints uncovered at the scene were Darlie's and her two children's'.

Investigator James Cron next detailed his search of a possible pursuer's flight through the Routier home, through the utility hall and garage, a very careful and scientifically based trek that failed to turn up clues of there ever having been an intruder. Summarizing, he said, "After my initial walk-through, I thought someone in the family had committed the murders and staged the scene. The further I got into my investigation, the more convinced I became."

Charles Linch, a trace-evidence expert, took the stand. Linch, an analyst for the Southwestern Institute of Forensic Sciences, supported Cron's claims. It was impossible, said he, for an intruder to have left the scene of the crime without leaving a trail of blood. Hammering this point home for the benefit of the court, the prosecution next delivered blood expert Tom Bevel, who professorially illustrated the velocity and direction of the blood found on

Darlie's nightshirt. His finding was that her sons' blood found on the nightshirt had been literally sprayed onto it while she was in the act of various upswing motions in other words, stabbing/slicing gestures.

The state's final witness after weeks of hard-hitters was the hardest hitter of all, the FBI's special agent Al Brantley. He first listed the reasons why he disregarded an intruder among them, that the screen would not have been cut, but removed, and that the positioning of the Routier house, on a cul-de-sac and with a high fence, would have discouraged a burglar or rapist.

He addressed motive. Had a thief called, Darlie's jewelry, which was in the open and very visible, would have been taken. And as for attempted rape, as Darlie had suggested sexual offenders assailing a woman would not have killed her children but used them as leverage to get her to submit.

And discussing the savagery expended on the young victims, he theorized that the attack was personal and done in extreme anger. Brantley concluded: "Someone who knew those children very well murdered them."

# The Defense

Routier, flanked by guards, enters court

By the time the defense opened its arguments, the case looked unsalvageable for its client. But, Doug Mulder and his team did the best with what they had to contradict and counteract the gallows material planted by Prosecutor Greg Davis.

Leading the defense's string of witnesses were friends, neighbors and relatives who had known Darlie for years and who vouched for her character. Reverend David Rogers, who officiated at the funeral, thought Darlie was "grieving appropriately." Friend Cara Byford spoke of

Darlie's kindness and of how Darlie came to her after the murders for consolation since Cara had lost a four-month-old boy years previously. Next-door neighbor Karen Neal saw Darlie's grief as real and not at all artificial as the prosecution tried to paint.

Husband Darin Routier's presence in the witness box brought attention as he admitted to family problems due to financial woes, but attested that his wife was truly devastated by their boys' deaths. He choked back tears when he recalled the morning of the murder and his administration of CPR to Damon. "Darlie was running back and forth getting wet towels, going 'Oh my God! Oh, my God, he's dead!' I blew two or three times. She was over him trying to hold the gaps in his chest together. I knew he was dead in three minutes. I screamed at Officer Waddell, and Darlie tried to get him to go to the garage. All three of us were in shock."

A major impact in the prosecution's case had been the "hesitation" wounds on Darlie's throat. But Bexar County's medical examiner Dr. Vincent DiMaio, a professor of forensic pathology, tried to lay doubt that the woman's wounds were self-inflicted and "surface". Her throat slash, he claimed, had come within two millimeters of the carotid artery. As well, he diagnosed bruises on her arms as mass trauma coming from a blunt instrument and not self-given.

Since the prosecution had made much of Darlie's contradictory testimony before and after her arrest, attorney Mulder needed a reliable witness to express, in medical terms, how a suspect, having faced psychological trauma, often lapses in and out of memory. He found that witness in forensic psychologist Dr. Lisa Clayton. The expert had done much work on the homicidal mind.

Dr. Clayton had interviewed Darlie and believed her to be innocent, stating that she showed the typical blackout and distorted-memory symptoms of people who lived through a trauma and were forced to give a clear description of their encounter.

The final witness for the defense on January 29 was a surprise and, as it turned out for the defense itself a bad move: the accused, Darlie Lynn Routier. Mulder had tried to talk his client out of appearing, insisting that she would pit herself against cross-examination by a ruthless prosecution team that could make mincemeat out of anything she said. But, Darlie persisted.

The moment started off well as Mulder guided her through her life story, her dedicated motherhood to three children, her domestic ups and downs; he had her skillfully read excerpts from her diary that penetrated the shell of what the prosecution called a wicked woman to display a thoughtful, sometimes deep, person who recognized and cherished life's values. She explained that the Silly String used at the graveside during Devon's posthumous birthday party was brought by her younger sister, Dana, not her, as a symbol of the fun the little boys would have liked had they been alive. She remembered the night of the murder, emphasizing that if her story changed slightly it was because she simply could not remember things clearly. The shock had left them jumbled.

But, when the defense stepped aside, the prosecution wilted her in the face of her own statements; they badgered and barked and condemned her. They wouldn't accept amnesia, they wouldn't accept alibi, they wouldn't accept a word she told them and drove into her with an inquisition. They asked about why she told one policeman one thing and something else to another; they asked why her dog didn't bark when the intruder entered the house, they asked why the kitchen sink was cleansed of its blood; they asked why she lied, lied, lied and when they left her alone, she was a sobbing, wretched woman for the jury to see.

# The Blood Evidence

The prosecution's case against Darlie Routier included bloodstain pattern analysis by Tom Bevel. The National Academy of Sciences has stated that this approach to crime scene analysis is "more subjective than scientific."

Darlie Routier's nightshirt

Testimony by Bevel contradicted the physical evidence in the Routier case. For example, Bevel testified that because bloodstains on the right shoulder area of Darlie's nightshirt contained a mixture of Darlie's blood and each of her two children (one stain contained Darlie's blood mixed with Devon's and the other contained Darlie's blood mixed with Damon's) it showed that Darlie had to have been bleeding when the boys were stabbed.

This testimony contradicts the state's case because of the sock, found about 75 feet down an alley way that ran behind the Routier home. The sock contained Devon and Damon's blood on it. This means that by the time the sock was deposited in the alley, the Routier children had already been attacked. However, the state never explained how Darlie could have gotten the sock into the alley without leaving a trail of blood leading to or around where the sock was found. As evidenced by the crime scene photographs, Darlie bled a great deal from her injuries.

The above is a major problem because the prosecution's own expert acknowledged she had to have been bleeding when she allegedly stabbed the boys. For the prosecution to have been correct, Darlie also had to have been bleeding when she deposited the sock (which we know because blood for each child was on that sock).

Location of the sock containing bloodstains

Another problem with the blood evidence is that Darlie's nightshirt was cut and removed from her while she was treated by a paramedic. Though special care should have been taken to preserve the bloodstains on the shirt it appears the shirt was eventually placed into a bag prior to being dried.

In addition, the chain of custody for the shirt, as well as the clothing removed from Damon Routier, is highly problematic. The clothing was placed into bags and taken to the fire station. The items were then retrieved from the station by police.

Officer Mayne testified that he picked up two paper sacks from the fire station. He said that he opened the bags and observed blue jeans and underwear in one, and Darlie's nightshirt in the other. Nowhere in the entire trial transcripts is there a description of which sack contained the shirt Damon was wearing when he was murdered. Was the shirt placed into the bag with the jeans or with Darlie's nightshirt? This question remains and is important because of the possibility of cross-contamination of blood from one item onto another.

Darlie's shirt was also put into a paper bag without being folded or dried. Mayne testified at trial that there was blood on the bottom of the bag indicating the shirt had wet blood on it when placed into the bag. This could have allowed blood to seep from one area of the nightshirt onto another. This means that the information garnered from any of the clothing was questionable simply due to the lack of a process used to protect the integrity of the evidence, and then also the problematic chain of custody.

The nightshirt should have been inadmissible for these reasons alone, and yet Tom Bevel was given the go ahead to testify about the two above-referenced stains on the shirt. A question that no one will ever be able to answer now is if those mixed blood stains were a result of cross-contamination. Moreover, did Bevel realize that such a serious problem existed regarding the clothing and possible cross-contamination?

# Tom Bevel

Tom Bevel

Tom Bevel, a charter member of the Scientific Working Group on Bloodstain Pattern Analysis (SWGSTAIN), has testified for prosecutors throughout the nation. His testimony has helped to secure convictions of many people. He helped to convict Tim Masters who was later exonerated in 2011 due to advanced touch DNA analysis. Richard and Selma Eikelenboom helped to demonstrate that the physical evidence retrieved from murder victim Peggy Hettrick did not match Timothy Masters. Instead, it matched Peggy's ex-boyfriend, Matthew Zoellner. Tim recently published a book about his experiences, with the help of coauthor Steve Lehto, called *Drawn to Injustice: The Wrongful Conviction of Timothy Masters.*

Tom Bevel originally testified that Peggy was murdered in the area where she was found. He later claimed that the prosecution had not shown him all the pertinent photographs relating to the case. Upon examining other existing photographs, Bevel stated that Peggy was murdered elsewhere and dumped in the location she was found. This was critical to Tim's case because police and prosecutors claimed the teenager (who was 15 at the time and did not have a car) murdered Peggy near his home and dragged her body further into the field.

Bevel was also involved in helping to convict Warren Horinek. The investigator, medical examiner, and district attorney all believed that Horinek's wife Bonnie committed suicide. However, Bonnie's parents disagreed and hired an attorney to help them obtain an indictment against Horinek.

At a later trial, Horinek was convicted based on Bevel's testimony that blood on his shirt came from him shooting his wife instead of from CPR efforts that Horinek was observed conducting.

As described above, Tom Bevel testified at Darlie's trial on behalf of the prosecution. Lloyd Harrell testified for Darlie's defense. He was employed with a private investigation firm. Before working as a private investigator, Harrell worked for the Federal Bureau of Investigation (FBI) as a special agent.

At trial he testified that the prosecution's transcript of the 911 call Darlie made to the Rowlett police on June 6 of 1996 was not accurate. He also discussed the secret wiretapping of Devon and Damon's grave site, by the Rowlett police, stating it was an unlawful act because it violated federal law. When asked if he had seen a warrant or other document authorizing the secret recordings, Harrell stated that he hadn't.

On December 30th of 1996, before Darlie's murder trial, Harrell met with Tom Bevel, Douglas Mulder, Richard Mosty, and Curtis Glober. He testified that Bevel made "materially different" statements during that meeting then the ones he made under oath and on the stand.

Bevel explained in the meeting that specific bloodstains had been picked for testing for several reasons. Harrell testified: "His first concern was that a stain must have directionality. He explained that directional means in a bloodstain that one axis of the stain is longer than the other one. From the axis he then can determine the directionality, whether the stain is up or down or sideways. In order to make a proper determination, he indicated he made every effort to sample a single stain as multiple stains may cloud the issue of directionality."

During the meeting, Bevel informed the attendees that one of the issues regarding the stains in question was that they contained a mixture of Darlie and her children's blood. As described above, the lab reports show that Darlie was the main contributor of each blood stain. Each individual stain contained a minor contribution from each of her children. There was no way to determine how the stains became mixed.

Bevel's statements during the December meeting were not in line with his later testimony at Darlie's trial. At trial Bevel attempted to suggest that the mixed bloodstains occurred due to two separate events involving cast off or blood spatter. Harrell was asked on the stand if he believed that Bevel's testimony was contradictory to what he told people in the earlier meeting. He said the following:

"Absolutely, for this reason: In Oklahoma City he was asked at least twice, does this mean that each of those stains, the knife tip had to contain the blood of Darlie and the blood of one of her children?" Harrell stated that Bevel's answer was "yes".

# Other Cases Involving Bevel

As discussed on the evidence page, Tom Bevels name comes up in other cases that are confirmed or suspected wrongful convictions. The following include cases Bevel has been involved in and the circumstances surrounding each.

Jason Payne (Texas)

Warren Horinek (Texas)

David Camm (Indiana)

The following are cases where people were exonerated after having been convicted at trials where Tom Bevel testified on the side of the prosecution.

Ron Williamson and Dennis Fritz (convicted in 1988; exonerated by the Innocence Project in 1999)

Timothy Masters

## The Knife

A separate, but seemingly related problem existed with the knife as well. The prosecution claimed that a single knife was used in the attack and that the knife came from inside the Routier home. However, when the knife in question was tested for DNA only Darlie and Damon's blood was identified on it. Devon's blood was not. The prosecution did not try Darlie for Devon's murder, however. They only tried her for Damon's.

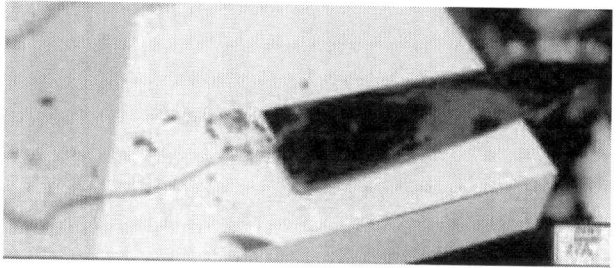

The knife with stains from Darlie and Damon's blood, but not Devon's

Some have said that prosecutor Greg Davis only sought a conviction against Darlie for Damon's murder because he planned to try her for Devon's if she was acquitted. However, this does not make sense because since blood from Damon was found on the knife, and blood from Devon was not, it means the state's case that Darlie committed the murders was stronger in Damon's case then Devon's. If the prosecution had been unsuccessful in getting a conviction for Damon's murder, they would have been even less likely to get a conviction for Devon's.

Due to Damon's age at the time of his murder, the offense qualified as a capital one. When convicted for the murder, Darlie received the death penalty. At least one juror has emerged to state that he now believes Darlie is innocent and that he made a mistake in his decision to declare her guilty.

**Bloody Towels**

Towels found in the living room and the hallway confirmed claims made by Darin and Darlie that she had gone into the kitchen to get towels and also wet towels in the sink.

# The Towels

Towels in the hallway

The presence of towels at the crime scene supported Darin and Darlie's claims regarding activity in the kitchen. At the bond hearing Darin testified that upon hearing glass break and Darlie screaming, he ran down the stairs and spotted Devon laying on the floor. He stated Darlie "grabbed the phone and then she was by the sink". Prosecutor Greg Davis asked Darin what he did next and he responded that he went over to Devon.

Davis asked, "When you came into this Roman room and you went to Devon, did your wife follow you over to Devon?" The Roman room is what the family called the living room where Darlie and the boys were sleeping the night of the murders.

Darin responded to Davis by saying, "Not at that point." Davis started to ask something when Darin added, "She went straight to the phone — she went straight to the sink to get towels." The phone was cordless. Darin and Greg Davis discussed the matter further:

**Davis:** All right. Where was your wife during the time that you were with Devon?
**Darin:** She was in the kitchen getting kitchen towels out of the thing. I could hear the water running, and then she took them over — and brought towels over to Damon.
**Davis:** So, you actually — is it your testimony today, that you actually saw her go to the kitchen sink?
**Darin:** Yeah.

Davis challenged Darin regarding the information, claiming he had not disclosed the above details to the police. Darin stated he had told the police Darlie went to the sink two or three times. He described spending approximately three or four minutes trying to give Devon CPR. In trial testimony he described Darlie attempting to hold Devon's wounds together while he performed CPR. He then told Davis that Darlie put a towel on Damon's back (something the police and paramedic would later say was not observed on Damon):

**Davis:** Well, at what point did she start to do something different?
**Darin:** Well, I don't really know. I mean everything I was seeing was when I was coming up, after I was giving, you know, trying to give CPR to Devon.
**Davis:** Well, you just told me that in the beginning that she was walking between the end of the kitchen bar and the kitchen sink, and I'm trying to understand at what point did that activity end?
**Darin:** Probably about the time that she came over to

Damon and gave him — you know, put a towel on him, she was pretty much at his feet, of me looking up and seeing him — you know, seeing her, seeing Damon laying on the floor, and me trying to work on Devon, you can't really put it all in perspective, it's just a lot of different things happening all at the same time.
**Davis:** Well, is it your testimony that she went over to Damon, and actually put a towel on his back?
**Darin:** She laid a towel on his back.
**Davis:** Did she leave that towel on his back?
**Darin:** I would assume so, yes, sir.

Darlie's testimony at trial matched Darin's claims about her going to the kitchen and getting towels. She also testified that she wet the towels.

Lead investigator James Patterson testified to seeing towels in the hallway as well.

**Mulder:** Mr. Patterson, when you went through the residence, with the other detectives on the walk through on June 6th, did you see some towels with blood on them in the den area?
**Patterson:** The towels I remember were in the hall.
**Mulder:** Towels in the hall. All right. How many towels did you see in the hall?
**Patterson:** I don't — I didn't count them.
**Mulder:** Were they bloody?
**Patterson:** There were some washcloths that had some blood on them, or had something that appeared to be like blood.
**Mulder:** Were they wet when you saw them?
**Patterson:** I don't recall if they were or not.
**Mulder:** Were you told that they had been wet?
**Patterson:** No, sir.
**Mulder:** Did you inquire as to whether or not they were

wet?
**Patterson:** No, sir.
**Mulder:** It didn't make any difference?
**Patterson:** It made a difference.
**Mulder:** She told you she put wet towels on the boys, didn't she?
**Patterson:** In her written statement.
**Mulder:** Did she ever tell you that she put wet towels on the boys?
**Patterson:** Well, in her written statement she did.
**Mulder:** All right.

The towels in the hallway are visible on the police crime scene video

Officer David Mayne took the stand to testify about his involvement in the investigation. He took photographs of the crime scene and helped to collect evidence. He explained on the stand that he had collected two bloody towels from the hallway in the Routier home. Instead of placing each bloody towel into a separate bag, Mayne combined them into one. Defense attorney Richard Mosty asked, "And you know better than to put two bloody items into the same bag?"

Mayne responded, "Well, they were collected together."

"But you know better than to do that, don't you?" Mosty repeated.

Mayne gave no response to his question and the trial transcript reflects this.

The defense also brought up a bloody towel that was located near Devon. The following occurred during Mayne's testimony regarding that towel and the officer's decision-making about what evidence was important. Mayne acknowledged that he had collected records pertaining to a headstone the family had purchased for a cat, but not the bloody towel near Devon. Referring to the records of the headstone Mosty asked:

**Mosty:** Okay. And so you collected it?
**Mayne:** Yes, sir.
**Mosty:** Now, this is at — is this the same time that you are making the decision that the bloody towel by Devon is not important?
**Mayne:** No, this was later on in the day, sir.
**Mosty:** This is after you have already decided the towel is not important, you decide that the cat burial is important?
**Mayne:** Yes, sir.
**Mosty:** Okay.

Darin's testimony confirmed that Darlie had been getting towels, but also that she brought them to him as he was trying to help his son. Defense attorney Doug Mulder broached the topic with Darin during trial:

**Mulder:** Where was Darlie?
**Darin:** Darlie was running back and forth, from the kitchen, over to Damon, and then she came over to Devon. And she was going "Oh, my God, he is dead."
**Mulder:** What was she doing in the kitchen?
**Darin:** Getting towels.
**Mulder:** Wet towels?
**Darin:** Um-hum. (Witness nodding head affirmatively.)
**Mulder:** Brought them to you?
**Darin:** Yes, sir.
**Mulder:** Where — how many times did you blow into Devon's mouth?
**Darin:** I blew into his mouth about — at least two or three times.
**Mulder:** Where was she when you were blowing into his mouth?
**Darin:** Right over the top of him.
**Mulder:** What was she doing?
**Darin:** She was trying to stop the bleeding. She was trying to hold his chest together.

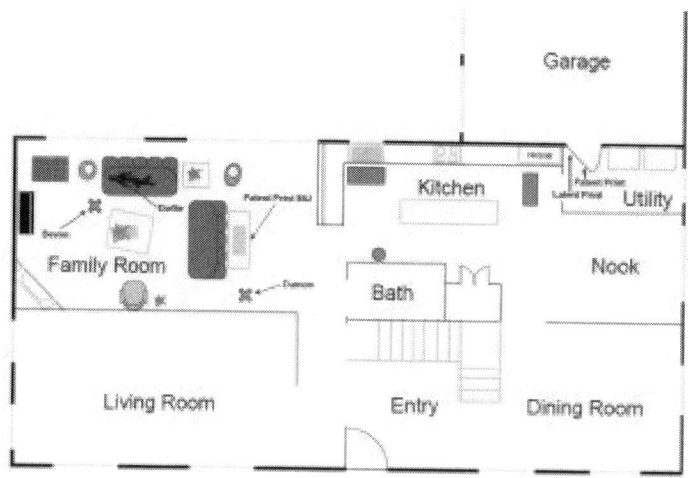

Layout of the first floor of the Routier house (hallway containing towels is between the "living room" and the "entry")

The above testimony was important for more than one reason, however. It confirmed that Darlie was attempting to assist in helping her children, as she and Darin both claimed; however, it also explained how blood from Devon and Darlie got on the sink handle. Darlie had readily admitted that she had wet towels. She had not received first aid training and was frantic. The police admitted, under oath, that they never asked Darlie about her going to the sink. Instead, they felt it was incumbent on her to disclose every detail pertaining to her actions that night.

But why would she have done that when the towels were in various places for anyone to see? Why point out to the police that she went to the sink when she thought the police were looking outside of the home for an intruder? Darlie had, after all, put in her statement that she had placed a towel on Damon's back. Darin claimed he *had* told the police more than once – the same police who consistently testified they did not take notes, did not always properly sign and date reports, did not bring their notes to trial the majority of the time (when they *did* take notes), and at trial could not always locate all of their reports and notes.

**Additional Photographs**

Defense exhibit 29 depicted towels in the hallway – one of which was obviously bloody.

Defense Exhibit 29

At least two additional photographs entered as exhibits by the defense depict a bloody towel located next to Devon. This image supports claims by Darlie and Darin that she went back and forth from the living room to the kitchen to get towels to assist in rendering aid to her children.

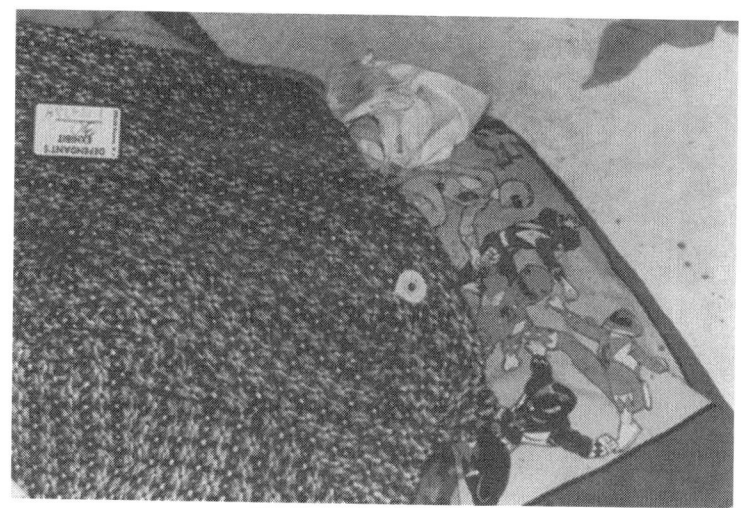

Defense Exhibit 30

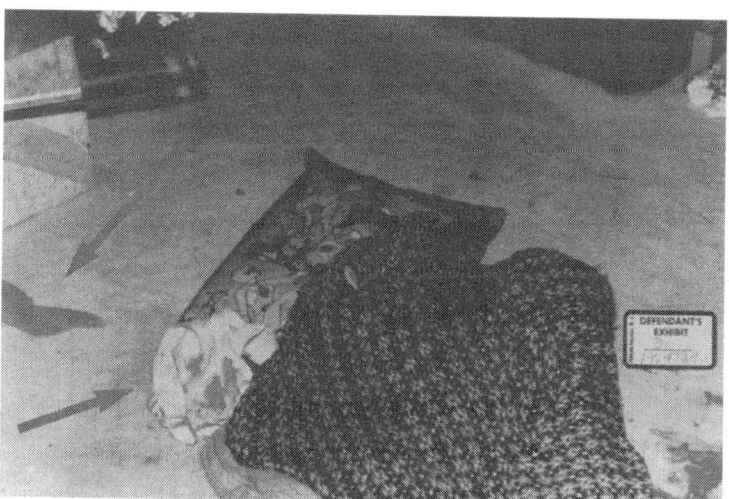

Defense Exhibit 31

**Darlie's Pillow**

The prosecution contended that Darlie cut her own throat while she stood at the kitchen sink. However, blood from Darlie's pillow (and the pillow cover) supports that her throat was cut while she was sleeping on the couch. Pictures of this evidence were entered as exhibits at trial, but the myth that there was no blood on Darlie's pillow erroneously persists to this day.

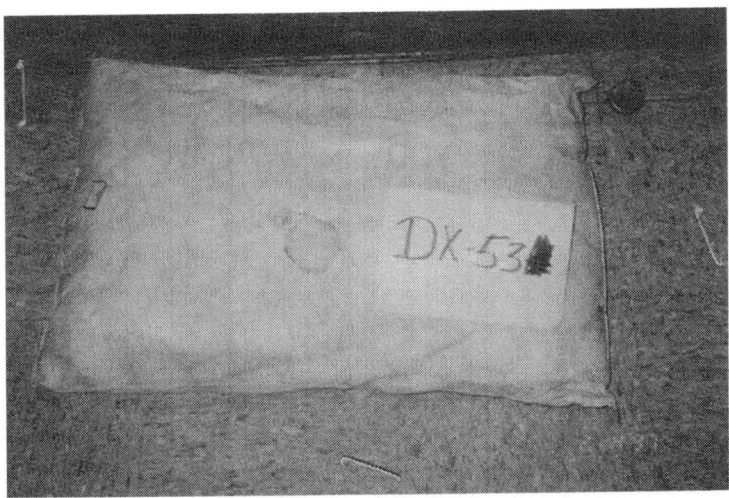

Darlie's pillow without the cover

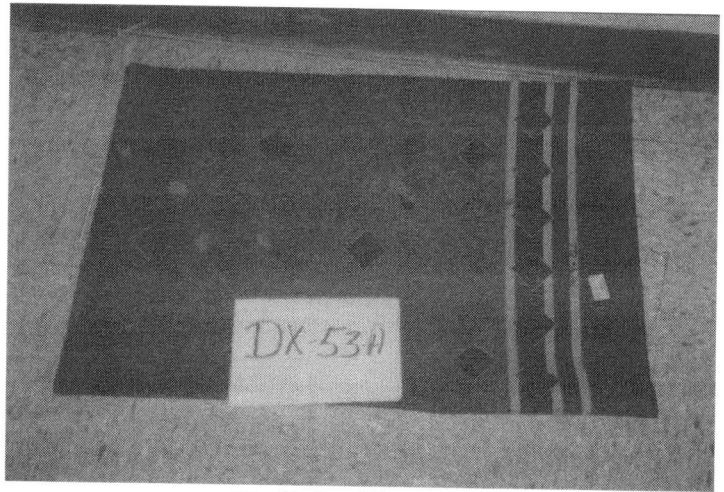

Darlie's pillow case

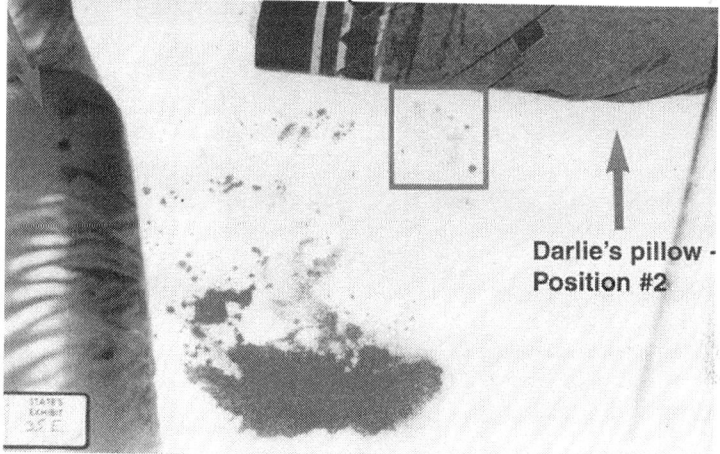

Blood is visible on Darlie's pillow here

The blood was mentioned at trial when defense attorney Richard Mosty questioned Charles Linch.

Mosty: Now, did you ever see this maroon pillow?
Linch: Yes, I did.
Mosty: Did you take that?

Linch: No, I didn't.
Mosty: Who collected that?
Linch: That was collected by the Rowlett Police Department.
Mosty: And, it had blood, it had — this maroon pillow had blood on both sides of it, didn't it?
Linch: Right.

# The Fingerprints

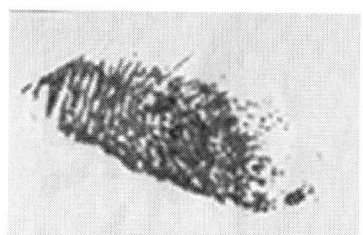

State's exhibit 85-J (the bloody print from the glass table)

Three fingerprints taken from the Routier home are of special interest. One of the prints was left in blood on the glass coffee table in the family room. A second bloody print was found on the utility room door. A third latent print was identified and lifted below the bloody print on the door.

A number of experts have excluded Darlie as the source of any of these prints. One expert, contracted by the prosecution, contends that one of Darlie's fingers cannot be identified or excluded as the source of the bloody print on the glass table. All other members of the Routier family, as well as officers and paramedics have been excluded. One of Darlie's appeals attorneys, J. Stephen Cooper, stated that a minimum of three experts have excluded Darlie as a source of that particular print.

Darlie has been excluded as a source of the prints on the utility room door. The federal appeals court has granted Darlie permission to have the prints run through existing fingerprint databases. Unfortunately, this process has been delayed until after the state of Texas conducts testing on other items.

# Shoe prints

We will examine this subject in greater detail, using court testimony and photographs to provide a more dimensional view of this particular evidence.

Much emphasis was placed on bare footprints which showed a path from the family room to the kitchen and back again. Those prints were identified as Darlie's. The prosecution suggested the existence of the bloody footprints disproved her claims about an intruder entering the home. However, both Darlie and Darin stated repeatedly that Darlie made trips into the kitchen to get towels and to wet them. Their claims were supported by the abundance of bloody towels captured in photographs and described in various testimonies.

Far less attention was paid to shoe (or boot) prints, and patterns of blood that resembled impressions of shoes or shoe prints, throughout the first floor of the home. These prints are especially important because if an intruder entered the home, evidence of the person or people's presence should have been detectable. Existing evidence supporting the belief that someone from outside the Routier home broke in, includes the fingerprints left in blood.

Given that the prosecution was attempting to discredit Darlie's repeated claims about what happened in her home, one would expect the defense to have spent more time assessing suspected or confirmed shoe prints within the home. The defense touched on these shoe prints during the bond hearing and the jury trial, but there is no evidence showing the defense did any testing or examination of their own to prove or disprove the prosecution's contention that any (or all) shoe prints in the home belonged to police and/or emergency personnel who entered the home.

Both Darin and Darlie were barefooted when the police responded to the home. Lieutenant Matt Walling testified at Darlie's trial that he checked Darlie and Darin's shoes for blood but did not find any. By contrast, Officer David Mayne testified he observed what appeared to be blood on a pair of Reeboks belonging to Darin. The shoes were collected as evidence and tested. Blood from the shoes matched Darlie. This is discussed in greater detail later on this page.

**The Garage**

Blood was observed in the garage. Charles Linch testified about seeing this blood during Darlie's bond hearing under cross-examination by Douglas Parks. Linch was advised by James Cron that the blood had not been there previously. The problem with this claim is that there was no proof at all that an officer had tracked in the blood. Parks questioned Linch about the blood in the garage at the bond hearing.

Douglas Parks: You indicated that you proceeded into the garage and saw some blood out there; is that correct?
Charles Linch: That is right.
Douglas Parks: Where was that?
Charles Linch: There is – as you come out of the utility room and take a left towards the window, there is a freezer. Down in that floor, there was some sort of sign, plastic sign, maybe this big and there was some – not a discernible blood footprint, but a light shadow of transfer smeared type blood.
Douglas Parks: Okay. Did it appear to be a footprint

transfer?
Charles Linch: It could have come from a shoe.
Douglas Parks: You indicated that you were advised that it was probably left by a police officer?
Charles Linch: I was advised that it was not seen earlier.
Douglas Parks: Who advised you of that?
Charles Linch: Retired Lieutenant Jim Cron with -

The sign is shown in State's exhibit 111-D. The writing and arrow were added.

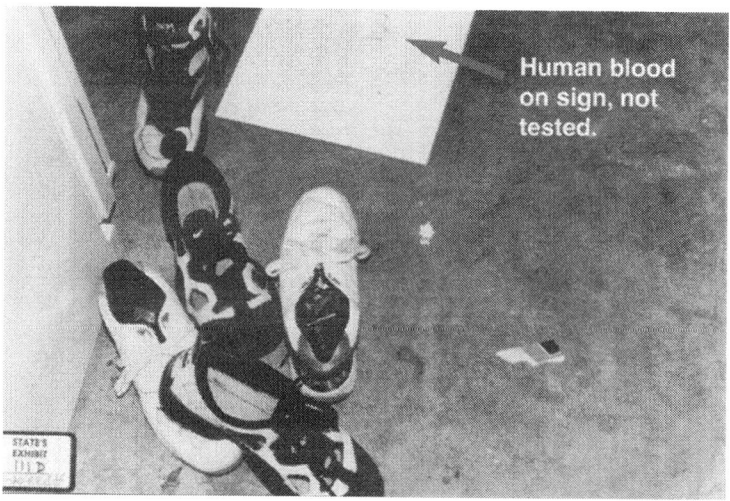

James Cron testified about a possible shoe or boot print on the floor of the garage as well. He described a single smudge of blood about two feet into the garage (from the utility room). He claimed it had not been there previously and dismissed it as having been tracked into the garage by one of the investigators. He surmised the transfer of blood occurred as a result of someone stepping onto a small drop of blood and then walking into the garage area. However, he was asked if he went back to check to see if it appeared a drop of blood had been stepped on and he said he did not.

The only proof the jury had that the blood was tracked in by an officer was Cron's testimony. This print was not investigated as though it were a part of the crime scene (which it well may have been) and it was not attributed to any particular investigator. It is also not entirely clear if Linch and Cron referenced the same print since Cron did not say anything about the sign Linch mentioned. Were they even referring to the same thing?

**The Utility Room**

The utility room and its doors have been discussed previously in reference to the bloody and latent prints obtained. These prints are visible in the following pictures.

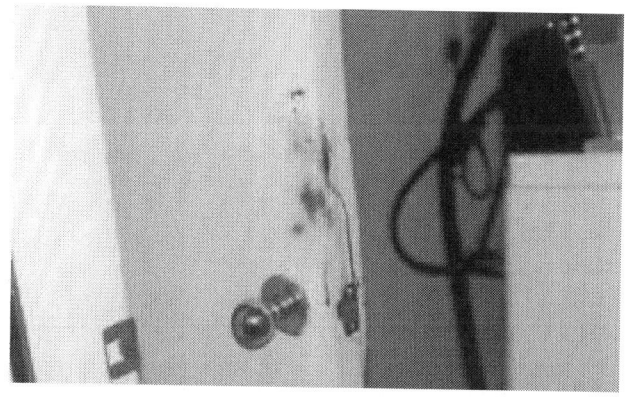

State's exhibit 38-B showed a smudge of blood that was found on the bottom part of the utility room door leading into the garage. The outline of what appears to be a partial shoe print can be observed on the floor, appearing as though the door had come in contact with a shoe.

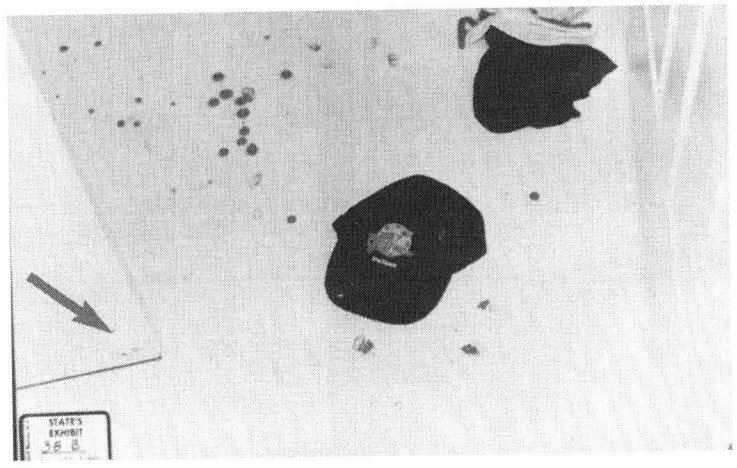

The picture has been enlarged and showed where an outline of part of a shoe may be seen. The smudge of blood is more readily apparent on the enlarged version of the exhibit.

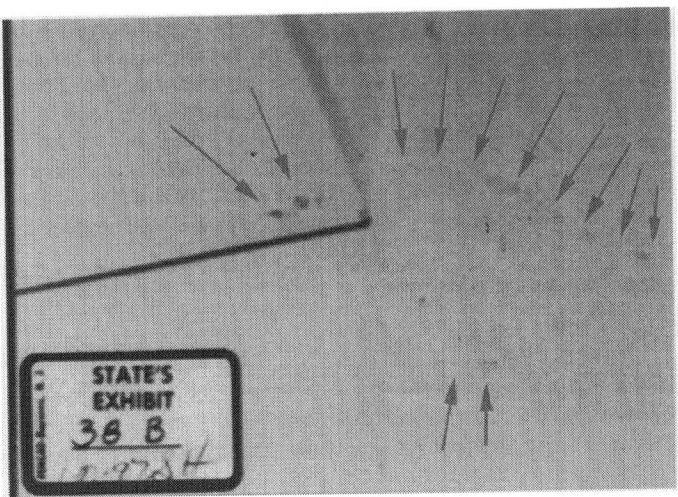

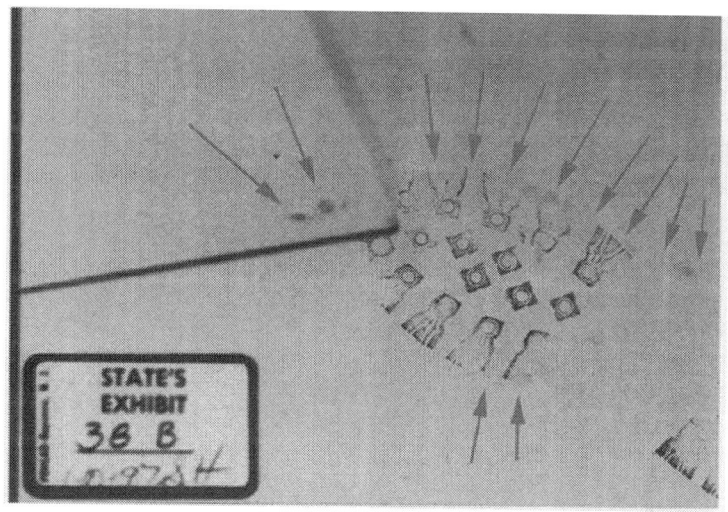

The bloody smudge from the utility room door was discussed at Darlie's bond hearing as well.

Douglas Parks: What about on the door itself, going into the utility room from the kitchen, do you recall seeing any blood there?
Charles Linch: Yes, sir, there was some – a transfer smear type on the inside surface, that also continued into the part of the door that fits flush with the door facing.
Douglas Parks: Okay. What about the door that leads from the utility room into the garage, did you see any blood on that door?
Charles Linch: Well, that was the door I was just talking about.
Douglas Parks: That was the door you were referring to?
Charles Linch: Right.
Douglas Parks: Okay. Did that blood smear on the door leading into the garage also have at least a partial bloody fingerprint?
Charles Linch: I don't recall. I was leaving the

identification and characterization of fingerprints up to the police personnel.

## The Kitchen

A partial bloody shoe print was observed in the kitchen of the Routier home. James Cron, who testified for the prosecution, discussed this print.

Greg Davis: Did you see bloody footprints that you believed to be of different sizes in the kitchen?
James Cron: No.
Greg Davis: Now, did you ever observe anything in the kitchen that you believed to be a bloody shoe print?
James Cron: There was a partial one. I did see one.
Greg Davis: Okay.

The partial shoe print found in the kitchen was measured and photographed.

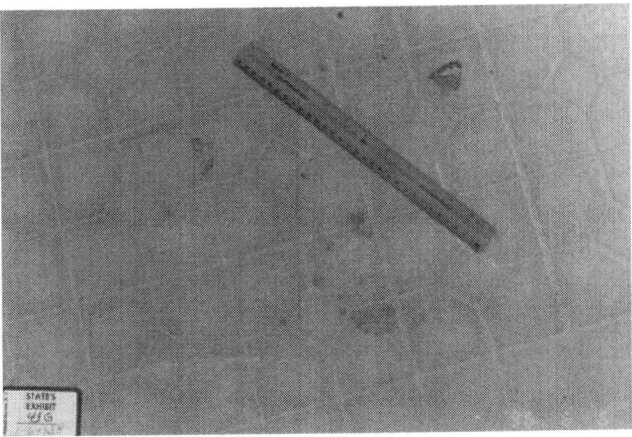

Cron also testified the print was consistent with the heel of one of Walling's shoes. The degree of consistency was not made clear in testimony except for Cron's claim that it matched the brand and style that Walling wore. There is no information available about what the defense did (or did not do) to confirm whether or not the print really was a close match to Walling's footwear.

**The Family Room**

At Darlie's bond hearing, Linch testified about what he believed was a shoe print behind the couch in the family room where Darlie and her boys were sleeping on the night of the 5th, going into the morning of the 6th.

Douglas Parks: Okay. In the den area, where the boys were found, besides blood and hair, did y'all collect any other kind of evidence?
Charles Linch: I asked – or it was done, that a strip of carpeting behind the couch, between the couch and the glass doors to the back yard, was cut up and collected.
Douglas Parks: Why was that?
Charles Linch: There were what appeared to be some foot impressions on it, bloody foot impressions.
Douglas Parks: From a bare foot or a shoed foot?
Charles Linch: I don't know.
Douglas Parks: Were photographs made of that?
Charles Linch: Yes, sir.
Douglas Parks: Have you done any testing on that piece of carpet since you had it cut out?
Charles Linch: I have not, serology, or DNA may have.
Douglas Parks: Is that in the kind of shape where you will be able to determine whether it was made a bare foot or a shoed foot?


Charles Linch: These were not distinguishable patterns. If it were a shoe, you couldn't include or exclude shoes, in my opinion. I would – the more I think about it, I would have the opinion that it was a shoe, more likely than a bare foot.

The carpet containing the partial shoe print was depicted in State's exhibit 81.

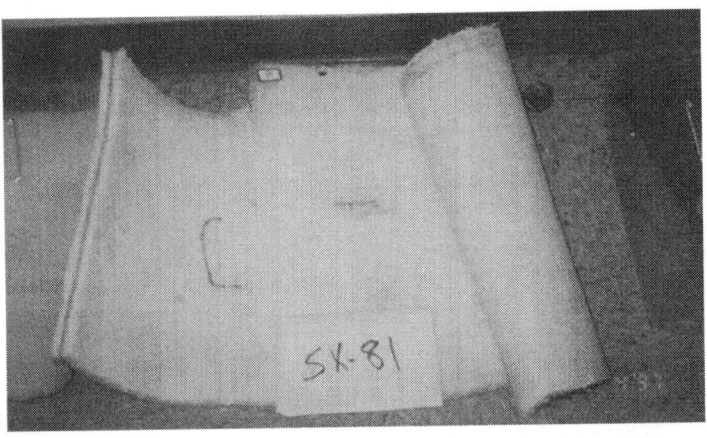

Officer David Mayne testified that he removed the above strip of carpet containing "a possible shoe print".

Where did it come from? Who left the print?

**Other Possible Shoe/Boot Prints**

The following is a picture of Defendant's exhibit 31, showing possible shoe prints left tracked in blood surrounding the area where Devon was photographed.

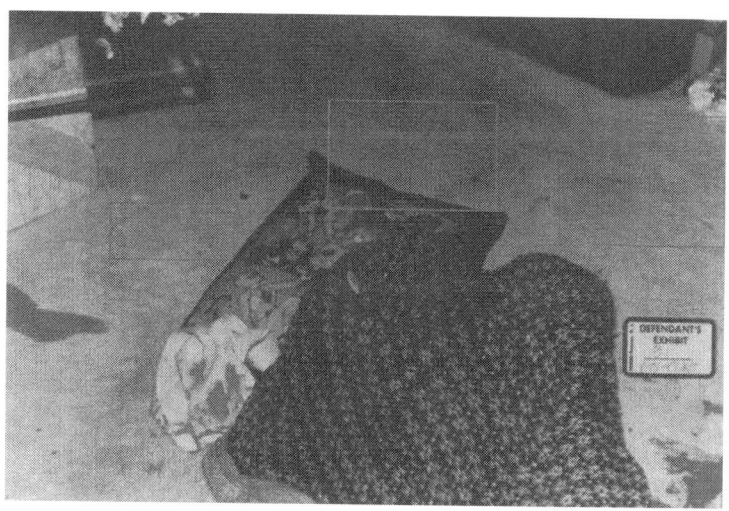

The following depicts a pattern that looks like a partial shoe or boot print.

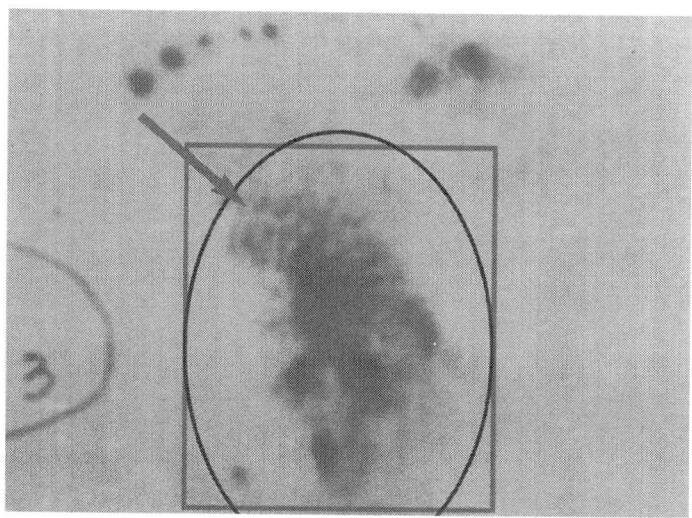

Another possible print on a rug from the Routier home

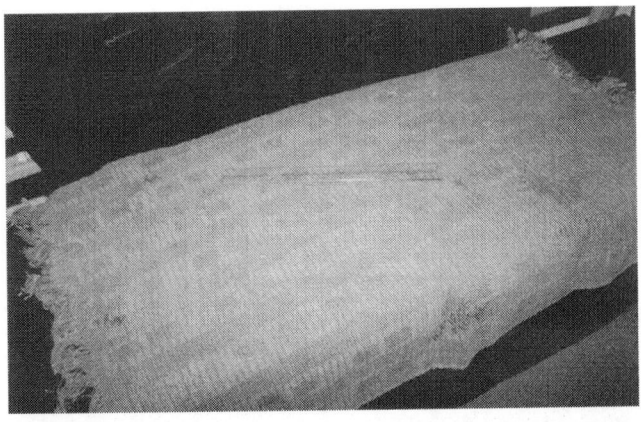

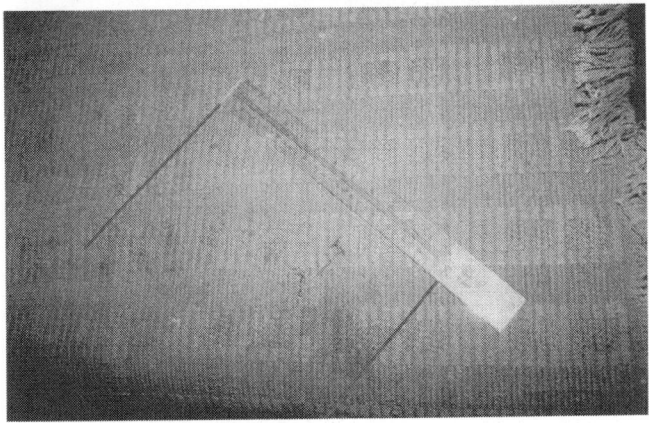

## Blood on Darin's Shoe

During Darlie's trial, various people mentioned a pair of Reebok tennis shoes. Officer Mayne collected the shoes when he observed what appeared to be blood on them. The shoes were tested and the blood matched Darlie.

The same shoes were mentioned not to incriminate Darlie in terms of the blood evidence, but rather to link the sock that was deposited 75 feet away from the home in an alley way. Photos of the shoes were entered into evidence as State's exhibits 71-A, 71-B and 71-C.

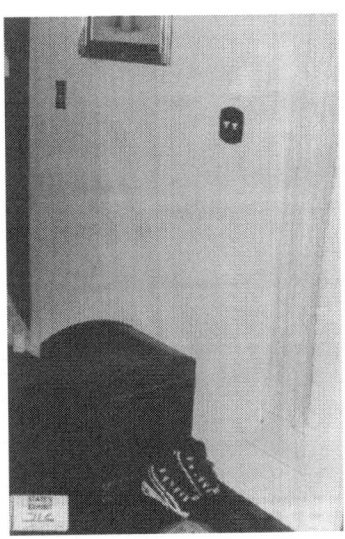

However, the shoes did not belong to Darlie. They belonged to her husband Darin. Greg Davis referred to the shoes as Darin's during his closing argument. Oddly enough, the defense did not refer to this physical evidence as a means of casting doubt away from Darlie and onto the only other adult living in the household. The same was true in reference to hair evidence found on the knife believed to have been used to stab at least one of the Routier children. That hair matched Darin also.

This is not to say that Darin committed the murders; this is to say that physical evidence in the case pointed away from Darlie and the prosecution ignored the physical evidence in favor of circumstantial evidence. The defense had an obligation to raise reasonable doubt in Darlie's case by emphasizing physical evidence that did not support the prosecution's theory, but there are clear instances where they failed to do this. This is one of them.

**Concluding Remarks**

Partial shoe prints were mentioned in the bond hearing and throughout Darlie's trial. Although the prosecution claimed to have matched one of the prints, found in the kitchen, to Officer Walling, there is no evidence the defense made any attempts to confirm this information. The defense also never appeared to follow up on matching any of the other partial shoe prints. The existence of the prints proves one of two things (or possibly both):

1. The crime scene was grossly contaminated by police (all of the shoe or boot prints cannot be attributed to emergency responders because they would not be walking behind the couch, nor would they have gone into the kitchen, utility room, or garage)
2. The shoe prints belonged to one or more intruders and were completely ignored as physical evidence

If the first scenario is correct it means that the crime scene was rendered unreliable by those charged with investigating it. As evidenced by exhibits entered throughout the trial, various items were moved around in between photographs. There is no question that the crime scene was contaminated. The only question is to what degree? Moreover, what evidence was lost or ignored as a result?

The existing shoe/boot prints warrant further examination.

Below is a map depicting the locations of some of the shoe/boot prints discussed above. A red foot print is used to denote the approximate locations of some (not all) of the partial shoe prints. The direction of some of the prints, such as the one behind the couch and by the patio doors and the one in the garage, are unknown. This map only depicts approximate location of the prints. The directionality of the print in the kitchen, located by the aisle, reflects Cron's testimony. There appeared to be more than one partial print in the utility room. Additional areas resembling partial shoe prints exist but are not all shown here.

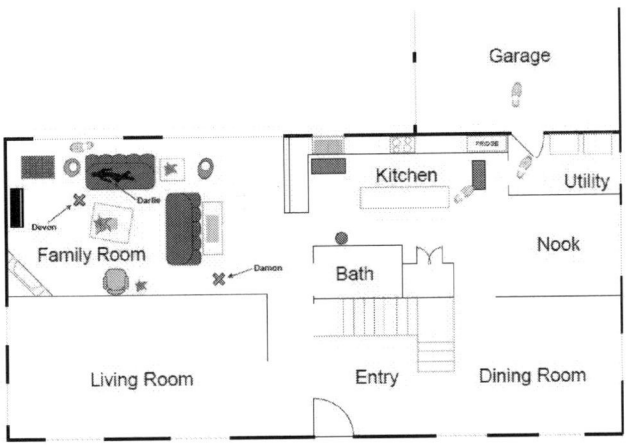

After hours of deliberation, the jury on February 1 found Darlie Lynn Routier guilty of the murder of her son Damon Christian.

Three days later, a somber Judge Tolle peered down from his bench to the white-faced Darlie before him, and read her the court's decided penalty. It was death.

# But: Is Darlie Innocent?

In all fairness, Darlie Lynn Routier, despite some extremely damaging evidence, may be innocent, say many. A special televised episode of *20/20*, entitled "Her Flesh and Blood," which aired on February 3, 2000, examined and updated the Routier case materials and found, among other things, that the jury may not have been shown photographs of bruises on Darlie's arms (which strongly indicated she fought off an intruder) nor the complete transcript of the court proceedings from which to make a final verdict. Indeed, the transcript that they did review contained, upon latter examination, 33,000 errors and omissions. As well, the audio tapes they heard were incomplete.

One juror came forth to admit he was peer-pressured into a guilty vote. On the televised program, he claimed he never saw the above-mentioned photos nor was the jury shown the police surveillance version of Devon's graveside birthday party that showed Darlie and her family sincerely grieving over the children.

On July 25, 2001, Holly Becka of the *Dallas Morning News* reported that Darlie's lawyers filed an appeal for her charging conflict of interest and 13 claims of trial errors: The appeal says that "she deserves a new trial because the judge didn't properly handle her lead defense counsel's conflict of interest in representing the only other suspect in the crime -- her husband." Her appeal doesn't implicate Darin Routier as the culprit but notes that inconsistencies in Darin's testimony could have prevented her counsel from correctly presenting information to the jury.

In early June of 2002, Dr. Richard Jantz, a fingerprint expert, indicated that the unidentified bloody fingerprint left at the crime scene is "consistent with an adult" rather than a child. This testimony supports Darlie Routier's claim that an intruder was present in the house at the time of the murders.

Later that month, Holly Becka of the *Dallas Morning News* reported that "Darin Routier asked his father-in-law (Robbie Gene Kee) whether he knew anyone who would burglarize his home as part of an insurance scam months before his sons were killed...Ms. Routier's family fears that Mr. Routier mentioned the plot to others, who broke in on their own. They say they think this is possibly why an intruder targeted the home." In fact, neighbors saw a black car watching the house before the Routier boys were killed.

In July, 2002, Darlie's lawyers argued that prosecutors should turn over evidence for new forensic tests. One item requested was the nightgown Darlie had on at the time of the murders. Her lawyers would like to conduct tests that they hope will indicate that her wounds were not self-inflicted. Defense lawyers also want to test the murder knife, the window screen and carpet samples.

Also, at this time, Darin Routier admitted that he had looked for someone to burglarize the family home to benefit from an insurance scam, but that he planned to have the burglary occur when the family was not at home.

The court may require up to 6 months to formulate its reply to Darlie Routier's request.

In the meantime, she sits on Texas' death row, waiting.

Is she one of the most heartless criminals in the state's history or a victim of an overly-aggressive prosecution?

# Divorce

In June 2011 Darin Routier filed for divorce, having remained married to Routier after the murder of their sons. Darin Routier stated that the decision to divorce was mutual and "very difficult," and that he still believes his wife is innocent. He went on to say that they decided on the divorce to move on from the "limbo" they've been in since her arrest and conviction.

# Innocence claims

Routier's family maintains a website which proclaims her innocence and a new site has been created by Routier's supporters to present their views and claims of her innocence.

Defense attorneys allege that errors were made during her trial and the investigation of the murders, especially at the crime scene. They also claim that there is significant exculpatory evidence which was improperly excluded, while questionable prosecution evidence was improperly allowed into evidence. Despite these claims, Routier's appeals have continually failed.

# Current status

Routier's appeals have been remanded to the state level for improved DNA testing. Once all state-level testing has been completed, the testing ordered by the federal courts will begin. Routier remains incarcerated on death row located in Gatesville, Texas at the Mountain View Unit of the Texas Department of Criminal Justice. She is assigned Department of Criminal Justice Identification Number 00999220.

# Over 14 years now-New 2012 Info

Darlie has no history of mental illness. She was not abusive to her sons. She was faithful to her husband and there is no fact from anyone saying differently on any of this.

The neighbors never saw them as wild though. She had kids in she baked cookies for and those kids stood up for her against the accusation that she killed her sons. Darin and Darlie helped out a cancer patient neighbor with a mortgage payment and seemed to have a heart. Whose idea was that, I don't know, but Darlie was baking the cookies.

All of a sudden their business went downhill and they got behind on their bills it is claimed; owing $10,000 in back taxes and $12,000 on credit cards. About a month before the murders Darlie considered suicide it is said by Darin and an incomplete diary entry. It was a fleeting thought apparently. My doctor once asked me if I had ever thought about suicide and my answer was, "Hasn't everyone?" He laughed, for it is true.

Maybe to different extents but if you know the word you have thought about it, if you have something you just think you can't face you may think about it, so I consider that pretty normal and nothing to even consider in anyone's sanity.

She had gone through the birth of a third baby and trying to get off a little extra weight and at that age I think many of us go through a little something anyway. Like did we make the right decisions in life, have we chosen the right path. Thirty is coming up and to twenties that looks old! It is nothing serious but a little something as I say and combined with all else going on with her she probably was suffering not abnormally from slight depression. That does not a murderer make.

# What didn't the jury know?

Never brought to the attention of the jury were other things of alarm and great importance included the pictures of Darlie's cuts and bruises on her arms taken when she was hospitalized the night of the murders. One juror told reporters he would never have voted to convict if he had seen the photographs. I would be sure others would have agreed. That is when I knew without a doubt! These are defense wounds, clearly.

A bloody fingerprint has been found that does not belong to Darlie, Darin, the children or any of the police or other people in the Routier house the night of the murder. This brings up some questions that need to be answered, at least in my mind.

"When they arrested Darlie, we just pretty much lost it," says Darin, and says they have never been able to grieve for their children but it is Darlie's husband and mother who have steadfastly continued the fight. They have appeared 10 times on nationally televised talk shows, printed up bumper stickers and have a toll-free phone number ( (888) 883-FAIR) appealing for donations and information that could help "find the real person who attacked Darlie and murdered her children." They have gathered support .Right now, they say, freeing Darlie is the only fight that counts.

Drake Routier looks just like his mother. The blue eyes, wide face, and his mother's mouth. The court took Darin's custody of the child, who was 7 months old at the time of the murders, simply because he defended Darlie! Is this

Texas law? His parents were allowed to raise the baby and he was given rights to visit him but still! Does this horror never end? If Darin is guilty of nothing how could they take custody of his child from him?

Darin and Darlie moved into her mother's home after the murders and lost the $200,000 house they built, also their 35-foot cabin cruiser, '86 Jaguar, plus some. Legal fees and bad publicity about the case ruined him financially. His electronics business, bringing a salary of $500,000 in 1995, lost 14 of its 17 clients and all employees.

There was many bad testimonies from people making Darlie look bad, there was no testimonies of the people who saw her much differently. Darin and Ms. Kee claim Darlie's trial mocked the judicial system. Evidence that would have cleared her was never presented, witnesses who could have contradicted the prosecution's assertions never testified, forensics testing was botched, depositions were distorted. Forensic fingerprint tests done after Darlie's trial still show that she is innocent of the crime for which she was convicted. A bloody fingerprint taken from her living room coffee table did not belong to anyone living in her home, and two more fingerprints in the utility room and door leading to the garage in which Darlie thinks the murderer escaped the Darin's home after attacking her and her two sons. No matter, repeated requests, the Court will not grant the evidential hearing necessary to investigate and evaluate this evidence.

Taken from the utility room door is a patent bloody fingerprint being the first print. Forensic fingerprint analyst Glenn Langenburg proved positively Darlie is excluded as the owner of this print. Darlie's exclusion as the source of this print indicates that an unknown third party not only deposited this print, but deposited it in blood, on the night of the murders.

The second print taken from this door is a latent print located below the patent bloody fingerprint. Latent print consultant Robert Lohnes checked this print in 2003 and said that it matched the second finger joint of Darin Routier on the middle finger of the left hand. In addition, Langenburg currently is conducting a second examination of the bloody fingerprint on the utility room door to determine whether Darin Routier can also be excluded as the source of this print. If, as Darlie expects, Darin Routier is not the source of this print, Darlie definitively will have demonstrated that an unknown third party deposited two separate fingerprints, one of them in the victims' blood, while fleeing the scene on the night of the murders. Darin Routier has admitted to trying to arrange an insurance scam, which included someone breaking into their home. He has admitted that he had begun the initial steps to arrange a break-in, but that it was to be done when no one was at home. No jury has heard this admission. Surely any law would be all over this, how many ways could this be the answer? Maybe not even the way Darin meant it to be but caused with unlawful schemes. I could understand them suspecting him, I really could, and why don't they? I don't believe Darlie would even suspect him, but if I were Darlie I would have to give that some serious thought, but I think Darlie either has a lack of intelligence or too much into herself, which does not equal a murderer.

The Birthday Party film that was viewed by the jury that made me think that is a killer, showed Darlie dancing on the graves of her son along with other family members, but did not show the hours previous to that scene when Darlie sobbed and grieved over the graves with her husband Darin. Why was the entire footage not shown?

Neighbors saw a black car sitting in front of the Routier

home a week before the murders took place. Other neighbors saw that same car leaving the area on the night of the murders.

There was talk the police did not protect the evidence as they gathered it possibly damaging its origins. Is this true? The screen investigators told the press it was cut from the inside being later proven in court to be cut from the outside. Things that make you say Hmm? Police investigated this? The investigators took the Fifth Amendment not talking, what were they afraid to say? You know without doubt they are hiding something. How are law witnesses allowed to take the fifth? On their deathbed will just one of them spill the truth?

When the paramedics arrived at the scene they said that Darin Routier was outside, but Darin was inside trying to save his children, so who was the man they thought was him? It was reported the testimony of the nurses was coached and rehearsed in mock trials by the prosecution prior to their testimony. Saying the cut in her neck was 2mm of the carotid sheath but external to the carotid artery was what Darlie's operating surgeons reported, and that the necklace she had on blocked the cut from going deeper, showing the seriousness and unlikely Darlie would or even could have done this herself.

Did debris on the knife in the kitchen get debris on it from police in the kitchen investigating the murder or did it come from the screen door? Darin's jeans had blood on them; no one should look into this? Darin Routier admitted to trying to arrange an insurance scam, which meant someone breaking into their home. He admitted that he had begun the initial steps to arrange a break-in, but that it was planned for when no one was at home. No jury has ever heard this admission! (Dear God! He is walking around free; he looks the guiltier of the two!) Sometimes I think children could run this world better. Does nothing enter their minds about this? Is it too late because they would be hanging themselves? Are they just that lazy?

The court reporter made mistakes in the manuscript so was there an improper read-back of testimony? Why is prosecution not forced to turn over evidence they have that should be available to both sides? Gee anyone who watches TV knows this rule. WHY? DNA testing could put many of these questions to rest. Why is there such a reluctance to do the testing? Many, such as people interested in writing Darlie's story have come to her side and since then have run into convenience problems seeing her or simply blocked!

# Judging Character

It is impossible to believe how much trouble the legal system will go to just to make things turn out the way they want. Just knowing the jury did not see this picture is enough to get the woman a new trial, but no. Not only did she lose two children murdered but now her youngest in all these years she cannot get back. So one day she may get out and a big settlement. What about the ones who do things like this? Shouldn't they be locked up? I think so!

I saw Darlie dancing around her children's graves; spraying silly puddy, laughing and acting so happy. I said to myself, "Of course she killed those babies", I was filled with hate, seeing her acting this way and those babies of hers, murdered and in the ground beneath her. I can't say that I accept this behavior even now, but people are different and I know they are, it still doesn't make them guilty of murder. I really felt so guilty the more I listened, read, and learned. I am not the only one with a change of mind.

With Darlie what I did not see was the same as others did not see, any proof, and how long will our rotten dirty judicial system keep getting by with having their say, right or wrong and hiding information to make things go the way they want? Why do they continually do this? What I and the jury did not see was Darlie's horrible cut and bruised black and blue arms and hands, defensive wounds, without any doubt.

I have read many true crime books and this is almost a common thing it has happened so often. The law wants to solve a crime so quickly some idiot decides how it happened and then makes sure it looks that way.

## There is no doubt here?

Darin Routier admitted to trying to arrange an insurance scam, where someone would be breaking into their home. He has admitted having begun the 1st steps to arrange a break-in, but that it was planned to be done when no one was at home. No jury heard this admission.

The screen which investigators reported to the press as being cut from the inside was later proven in court to be cut from the outside.

Was there an improper read-back of testimony to the jury by the court reporter, due to mistakes she made in the transcript?

The attorney that represented Darlie Routier at trial had an apparent conflict of interest, because he was said to have had prearrangement with Darin Routier and other family members not to pursue any defense that could implicate Darin. This attorney supposedly stopped key experts for the defense from finishing forensic examinations.

Also of concern, which were never brought to the attention of the jury, comprised the pictures of Darlie's cuts and bruises on her arms which were taken when she was hospitalized the night of the murders. At least one juror told reporters he would never have voted to convict if he had seen the photographs.

The prosecution has reportedly refused to provide access to any evidence in their custody in the case. Why is it not readily available to all interested parties?

The advancements in DNA testing could put many of these questions to rest. Why is there such a reluctance to do the testing?

Some writers who have interviewed Darlie Routier have decided to help her fight to get a new trial. Since reporting their opinions on her situation, they report that their ability to visit her has been blocked or made so inconvenient that little can be accomplished.

During the trial investigators invoked their Fifth Amendment rights against self-incrimination during cross examination, preventing the defense from rebutting their testimony. Why? This alone would be reason for disbelief and a new trial!

# July 3, 2013

Darlie's son Drake was diagnosed with Leukemia. He is undergoing chemotherapy. His family and friends are asking people to join in a prayer chain on his behalf. They have created a Facebook page to spread the word.

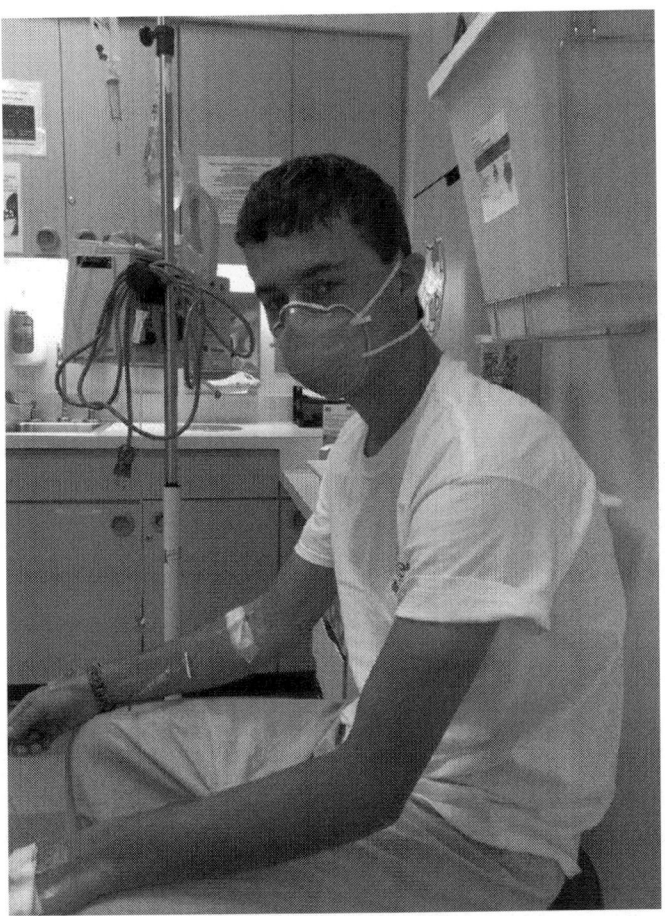

Darlie's son Drake

# In Closing

Darin Routier holding his son Drake at Devon and Damon's grave

**Life without parole should be new standard**

*"He needs killing"*.

For too long, Texas has abided by this bit of folk wisdom. Those who would kill need killing.

In theory, the ultimate punishment is imposed for the most heinous of crimes. But in practice, the death penalty has not been applied flawlessly or fairly. About 2 percent of known murderers are sentenced to death, but the fate of the accused often hinges on disparate details unrelated to the crime committed.

Wealth, race and random luck play a role in determining whether a case ends in death. Politics and geography can mean the difference between life in prison or lethal injection.

State-sanctioned death, it seems, is arbitrary.

Some of the most infamous murderers of our time sit in prison while lesser offenders are sent to die.

The Green River Killer, Gary Ridgway, confessed to killing at least 48 women but struck a deal to spare his life.

Juries sentenced Terry Nichols, accessory to the Oklahoma City bombing, and Lee Boyd Malvo, the "D.C. sniper," to life in prison.

Eric Rudolph, who bombed an abortion clinic, and Dennis Rader, the BTK serial killer, accepted plea agreements to avoid death sentences.

Our justice system has developed a dual standard, alternately meting out the death penalty and life in prison in comparable cases. In fact, some who conspire to commit the same crime are punished quite differently. Consider the teenage trio convicted in the murder-for-hire of Fort Worth socialite Caren Koslow.

Stepdaughter Kristi Koslow masterminded the gruesome killing and recruited her boyfriend and an acquaintance to carry out her plan. She was sentenced to life in prison. Brian Salter agreed to testify against his girlfriend in exchange for a life sentence. Jeffrey Dillingham exercised his right to a fair trial and was sentenced to die. Mr. Dillingham sought clemency, claiming a disparity of punishment. His request was denied, and he was executed in 2000.

We need a consistent standard.

But as long as capital punishment remains an option, it will be viewed as the ultimate goal, and prosecutors will face pressure to meet that goal.

Justice demands a punishment that is fair yet revocable, one that provides a sense of finality while allowing for the fallibility of the system.

It's harsh. It's just. And it's final without being irreversible.

Call it a living death.

Thanks to a recent change in law, Texas juries now have the option of imposing life without parole in lieu of the death penalty.

Across the country, public sentiment has begun to shift as legislatures have given juries this option.

Last year, for the first time, Gallup Poll respondents favored life in prison without parole over the death penalty, if given the option.

DNA exonerations have raised the specter of executing an innocent man. Questions about lethal injection methodology and mounting evidence exposing the arbitrary application of the death penalty also have helped bolster support for life without parole.

Locking away murderers for life would save states millions of dollars on costly death penalty appeals. And there is growing support for life without parole and putting convicts to work to pay restitution to their victims' families.

Death does not provide an added level of justice. A prison sentence that does not allow for the possibility of parole accomplishes the same objectives: protecting society from violent criminals and ensuring that every day of a murderer's life is a miserable existence.

Our standards of punishment have evolved over time, from the gallows to firing squads, from the electric chair to lethal injection. Life without parole, essentially death by prison, should be the new standard.

In the case of Darlie Routier, I believe that had the jury heard and seen all of the evidence she would not be on death row today. I have been a strong believer in "Innocent until Proven Guilty". But my feelings are even stronger on the fact that a person deserves a fair trial. And unfortunately, I don't see that Darlie Routier received her fair trial. I hope that one day the Texas court system will let her get her fair day in court.


If you wish to show your support to Darlie you can visit her Facebook page:

# facebook.com/darliefacts

# Look for these and other great books By David Pietras

From "Mommy to Monster"

The "Daddy Dearest" Club

The Manson Family "Then and Now"

When Love Kills

The Making of a Nightmare

THE INFAMOUS "FLORIDA 5"

Death, Murder, and Vampires Real Vampire Stories

The Life and Death of Richard Ramirez, The Night Stalker (History's Killers Unmasked Series)

Profiling The Killer of a Childhood Beauty Queen

No Justice For Caylee Anthony

A Texas Style Witch Hunt "Justice Denied" The Darlie Lynn Routier Story by

The Book of Revelations Explained The End Times

Murder of a Childhood

John Gotti: A True Mafia Don (History's Killers Unmasked Series)

MURDERED FOR HIS MILLIONS The Abraham Shakespeare Case

The Son of Sam "Then and Now" The David Berkowitz Story

A LOOK INSIDE THE FIVE MAFIA FAMILIES OF NEW YORK CITY

Unmasking The Real Hannibal Lecter

Top 10 Most Haunted Places in America

40 minutes in Abbottabad The Raid on Osama bin Laden

In The Footsteps of a Hero The Military Journey of General David H. Petraeus

BATTLEFIELD BENGHAZI

CASE CLOSED The State of Florida vs. George Zimmerman THE TRUTH REVEALED

CROSSING THE THIN BLUE LINE

THE GHOST FROM MY CHILDHOOD A TRUE GHOST STORY ABOUT THE GELSTON CASTLE AND THE GHOST OF "AUNT" HARRIET DOUGLAS...

Haunted United Kingdom

In Search of Jack the Ripper (History's Killers Unmasked Series)

The Last Ride of Bonnie and Clyde

The Meaning of a Tragedy Canada's Serial Killers Revealed

MOMSTER

Murder In The Kingdom

The Shroud of Turin and the Mystery Surrounding Its Authenticity

The Unexplained World That We Live In

The Good, The Bad and The Gunslingers

MOMSTERS Mothers Who Kill Their Children

KIDNAPPED A Parent's Worst Nightmare

Saving Angels

The Ghosts of Shawshank

The Tragic Little Pageant Princess

FOREVER MANSON

Made In New York City

Made in the USA
Lexington, KY
30 November 2014